TableTalk

TableTalk

HEARING THE SILENT FEAR
AND BRIDGING THE GAP

SHARI MOSS AND
MEGHAN FITZPATRICK

LIONCREST
PUBLISHING

TABLETALK

Hearing the Silent Fear and Bridging the Gap

ISBN   978-1-5445-1054-5 *Paperback*

        978-1-5445-1055-2 *Ebook*

        978-1-5445-1056-9 *Audiobook*

This book is dedicated to my two favorites: P.A.M. and Scott

And to Shari: thank you for all that you are—you're the raddest!

—MEGHAN

This book is dedicated to two of the bravest women I know: Pattie Canova for speaking out loud what is true and right for us all, and Meghan for laying her heart on the Table for her generation.

To Nicole for her assistance and audacity. To Michael for being so proud bringing them to my Table.

—SHARI

Contents

How cruel not to allow people to pursue what appears proper and beneficial to them. Yet in a sense you prevent them from doing just this when you are irritated at their mistake, for they are certainly drawn toward what seems proper and beneficial to them. "But they are mistaken," you might say. Then teach and enlighten them, but don't be irritated.

—FROM *THE ESSENTIAL MARCUS AURELIUS*
BY JACOB NEEDLEMAN AND JOHN PIAZZA

Introduction

TAKE A SEAT

They were straight out of luck, shit out of options, and burning up financial runway fast. Freshly graduated from college, unemployed and underemployed, unengaged and uninspired, Stella and Sam had found themselves where they never thought they would ever end up: lost, confused, underemployed, uninspired, and very alone.

At twenty-four years old, Stella drove to her nanny job every day at a quarter past eight in the morning. She drove with white fists and a clenched jaw. Despite the fact that she had what her friends called an "easy" job, Stella couldn't help but feel stressed.

She was stressed because ever since she'd graduated

college, she felt like she was stuck in a rut. Stella spent her days cleaning up after toddlers and her nights on the couch next to her mom. She went out with her friends on the weekends, partying way too hard to get her mind off of her current stagnation. She had been doing that for months, and it was getting old fast. Try as she might, she couldn't seem to get out of the nanny gig and into a "real" job. She had sent in 321 resumes to countless companies over the course of the previous year. She had heard back from five. They were all "nos." A couple of the responses said she "wasn't a fit," but to "try again later."

Stella was at her wit's end, and she felt that time was surely running out on her. Her parents told her to "stop being so dramatic," but Stella couldn't help the way she felt.

Stella says, "It was bad enough that I hated how bored I was as a nanny, but at least I was trying to get out. I just couldn't get a break. The more rejection [I had], the worse I felt, and the longer it was going to take me to do anything."

Stella couldn't help but feel that the momentum she had in high school and college had suddenly grinded to a halt. She wasn't able to enjoy the small victories or life outside of her struggle to find a "real" job. She constantly feared that she would never move forward. Her relationships with her friends suffered. Her relationship with her parents suffered. Her self-confidence plummeted. So, she stopped sending out resumes. Instead, she told herself that this was it and she better get used to it. But it was difficult for her to accept that because she still felt like she was missing out on "the best years of [her] life."

Sam had found himself in a similar position. He was also fresh out of college and feeling the same sort of stress that Stella felt. The difference between them, however, was that Sam had a "real" nine-to-five job. When we asked Sam what he did for work, he looked at us long and hard and said, "You know, I don't really know. I usually lie and tell people I do 'sales' or 'marketing,' but honestly, I mostly just sit around talking with coworkers and waiting for my boss to email me to run an errand or complete a spreadsheet."

When asked how the realities of this job lined up with what he thought it was going to be going into it, Sam said, "I was told this job was going to be fast-paced. I was told that I would get training and mentoring. I haven't gotten that. I guess I was naive. But come to think of it, I have friends in their first jobs who do get those things. So, I think it's just my situation." Sam admitted that during the day he "does a whole lot of nothing." Sam took the job hoping for a challenge...something to keep him interested or at least working all of the time. He had always kept to a rigorous schedule full of classes, clubs, friends, and team sports.

But now, he was having difficulty mustering the energy to do anything after 6:00 p.m. rolled around. It was making him seriously depressed. He knew there was something wrong with him. "Why couldn't I just get over it and like my job?" he wondered.

When asked how he dealt with those feelings, Sam said that he initially reached out to friends, but he felt that was "pretty pointless." He wasn't getting any direction out of those conversations, so slowly, he stopped talking about it altogether. Sam hadn't talked to his parents about it, because he knew that they'd tell him to "man up." Sam dealt with his frustrations, boredom, and feelings of depression alone.

Sam and Stella's stories might sound familiar to you. Sam and Stella might sound like your friends, siblings, or significant others. They may sound like your children. Or, they may sound like you.

We bet that if you changed a few details, you could insert yourself into Sam's or Stella's situation.

If you can, that is okay. You are not alone. The feelings of inadequacy, the anxiety, the periods of emotional turmoil, and the nagging voice that tells you that "you don't know where you are going, and you are falling behind" are all symptoms of what is commonly referred to as a quarter-life crisis. It's the hot new thing—everyone's doing it!

Research by a team of British psychologists from the University of Greenwich has shown that 86 percent of the people between the ages of twenty-five and thirty-five will experience one.[1]

Some experience a quarter-life crisis in their personal life, and some feel it in their professional life. A team of researchers from Ohio State University followed study participants from the ages of twenty-five to thirty-nine, periodically assessing their feelings of satisfaction in their work. "About 45 percent of participants consistently reported feeling lower than 'very satisfied' when it came to job satisfaction. Another 23 percent trended downward as the years passed."[2]

Sam and Stella represent a large portion of twenty-somethings who feel paralyzed and disconnected from their lives and who desperately want out. They are not alone, and you are not alone.

Perhaps your work life is lacking because you are unemployed or working part-time and searching for something more. In 2016, the unemployment rate for eighteen- to twenty-nine-year-olds was 12.8 percent.[3] Not only that, but there are an additional 1.8 million young adults that are not counted by the US Department of Labor in that statistic, because they have given up looking for work.

Compare this unemployment rate to the national average

unemployment rate of 4.9 percent.[4] Even more staggering, consider the unemployment rate during the Great Depression where "25 percent of all workers and 37 percent of all nonfarm workers were completely out of work."[5]

Unemployment creates not only financial tension, but also emotional and psychological damage. Stella and many others like her find themselves in a vicious cycle of depression and anxiety that leads to much deeper damage than just a gap on a resume.

Maybe you are like Sam and millions more who are underemployed. According to a report conducted by the consulting firm, Accenture, in 2016, 51 percent of millennials reported being underemployed.[6] Compare that to a report from the Federal Reserve Bank of New York, which found that the underemployment rate for all college graduates ages twenty-two to sixty-five has held steady at around 33 percent for the past three decades. For recent college graduates ages twenty-two to twenty-seven, the numbers have been rising steadily, with the underemployment rate rising to 44 percent in 2012. Compared to the unemployment rate, which fluctuated from anywhere between 4 percent and 10 percent during the same time period, "these numbers are alarmingly high."[7]

Underemployment is marked with feelings of shame and the constant wondering, "What am I doing wrong?"

Maybe you feel stuck because you just want to grow in your profession or industry, but you don't know how to. You attend networking events and read all the right books, but nothing ever comes of those experiences. Maybe you rarely reach out to the connections you make, or if you do, they fizzle out fast. Maybe you don't act on the advice you read in books, because it is difficult to apply in the real world.

For both Stella and Sam and millions of other twenty-somethings in America, the realities of their employment are personally damaging. They feel lost, stuck, confused, helplessly useless, rudderless, and without direction.

So, where do they turn? They might drown themselves in social media to distract themselves day in and day out. They may complain to their friends or their parents. They may see a therapist. They may still chip away at the obstacle blocking them from their fate by sending out an endless stream of resumes into the void, like Sisyphus and his boulder. Or, they may internalize their negative and discouraging feelings, build a wall around themselves, and hope they don't crack.

There is another way, though. It is not an instant fix. It is not a Band-Aid. It requires intentional effort. But once you get the hang of it, it gets easier and it works. If you do it right, it will help you get back on your feet, navigate the complexities and subtleties of adult life, and prepare you for professional and personal success. No resume required. No GPA minimum. No references needed. No cover letters, no applications. Just a plain and simple methodology to help you get to the place you want to be and become the person you want to be.

Sit down at our table. We invite you to join the conversation.

PART I

Come to the Table

CHAPTER 1

Come to Our Table

Maybe you're like Stella and Sam and have felt lost since leaving the structured routine of school.

Maybe you're like Sam, and you feel lucky to have a job that pays the rent when so many do not, but you still feel unhappy and unfulfilled. Maybe you feel guilty about this.

Maybe you're like Stella, and you can't talk to friends or parents about your feelings of inadequacy. All you can think about is how you're just spinning your wheels and going nowhere.

Maybe you are like Sam, who had so much fire in his belly, but it is now extinguished.

Maybe you're like Stella, and you can't seem to figure out

how to crack the code on the job search, and you wonder, "Am I just not good enough?"

Maybe you know a Sam or a Stella, and you want to help him or her.

We got you.

INTRODUCING MEGHAN

I felt like I was both Sam and Stella in the time leading up to and (a long time) after college graduation. While in college, I kept my nose down, participated in clubs and a community-service fraternity, and took part in internships. By all accounts, mine especially, I was ready to kick ass once graduation rolled around. As graduation approached, like my classmates, I readied myself for my uncertain future. I applied to jobs, internships, programs, and scholarships. Rejection after rejection hit my inbox. Many of the places I applied to never even bothered to reject me—they just never said anything. As the months wore on, and my graduation day loomed closer, I completely lost confidence.

April came and went, and although I continued to apply to positions, my confidence took a dramatic turn for the worse. I told myself that I didn't deserve to be fulfilled or feel successful. "Why even try anymore?" I wondered. I felt like

I wasn't "smart enough," "worthy enough," or "prepared enough" to have any sort of status in my postcollege life.

Writing this now, I see that I had fallen into destructive black-and-white thinking. No job? I was a failure. No call-backs? I probably don't deserve them. No one to turn to for help? I had no support network (or so I thought). But at the time, that was all I could focus on. Back then, I didn't have the perspective I do now. Today, I don't have the perspective that I will have decades from now.

May 14 rolled around. It was the last day of school and the last day of the lease on my apartment. The only other place to go was back home. So, I packed up my things and went home to California to live with my mom. I was the picture of success!

After a couple of days of wandering around my mom's house in my sweats, I forced myself to look at my savings. I was one of the lucky ones; I wasn't in debt from college. I wasn't in the red; in fact, I was sort of doing okay. I had saved a lot over the previous four years from my intern-ships and hospitality jobs. Plus, I am a frugal person (my favorite clothes are the ones I steal from my little sisters). I labored over some simple addition and figured that I could stretch out my money for some time.

For the next fifteen months, I wandered. I wandered in

and out of my mom's house, in and out of dead-end jobs, but mostly, in and out of trains, planes, rickety old busses, and hostels around the world.

I told few people about my whereabouts. Of the handful who knew what I was up to, some thought I was crazy, but most of them thought my life was "cool." I heard a lot of people, especially people stuck at a desk at their nine-to-five jobs, tell me they were "jealous" of my postcollege life. In response, I usually replied with something like, "Yeah, it's great." What I really meant to say was, "Yeah, it's pretty badass that I don't have to wear a suit or a uniform, but I'm terrified, lost, and not going anywhere—help!"

That time in my life was great, but not for the reasons you would think. It was difficult, exhausting, and intimidating. I learned a lot about the world and about myself. My emotions stretched to a limit I didn't know existed. But really what it was, more than anything, was cowardly.

You know that phrase by J. R. R. Tolkien that goes, "Not all who wander are lost?" Yeah, well, I was lost. I didn't wander because I wanted to. I wandered out of fear, desperation, and because I felt that I didn't deserve to do what I wanted. Even if I tried, I wouldn't succeed anyway. I was the twenty-two-year-old equivalent of the five-year-old who packs a suitcase and "runs away from home" by walking over to the neighbor's house and hiding in their backyard. I didn't know what I wanted, exactly, but I knew I wanted to be productive and helpful to someone. But somehow, I had convinced myself I was not worthy of that.

During those fifteen months, I carried a single thirty-liter backpack. But don't let that fool you—I was carrying two tons of emotional baggage.

I rarely talk about that time now, but if you asked me years later about the experience, I would say that I'm glad it happened. I'm thankful for the people I met and the experiences (the good, the bad, and the ugly) that I had. But still, it makes me shudder to think that I really felt that was my only way forward.

The first years of my twenties may or may not be unique, but the feelings I had are so common. Stella and Sam had them and so might you.

I was physically lost, but so many of us are personally and professionally lost as well. I was like Stella—struggling to find a place. She and I both desperately wanted a seat at the table of life, but for some reason (maybe for many reasons) neither of us had one.

When I returned from traveling, broke and tired, I opened up my familiar "Job Hunting" Excel spreadsheet and began sending out my resume once again. After months

of searching and working part-time, I got a single accep-
tance. I was ecstatic and felt like I had finally found my
way forward.

Sadly, soon after I started, my days began to feel empty.
Like Sam, I found myself with very little to do. The company I worked for was bloated: too many people for too
little work. My coworkers and I sat around most days,
waiting for direction, a project, or a task—anything to
come our way. After weeks and months passed, we collectively began wondering, "Is this really it? Why are
we here? We aren't helping anyone, and we sure aren't
helping ourselves." We did, however, become really good
at Ping-Pong!

At that job, I felt that I had finally gotten a seat at the
table—I was in! But like Sam, I realized that this place
wasn't my place. I may have found a seat at the table, but
that table was not my table.

Then I met Shari.

Shari came into my life unexpectedly through a work
project. We bonded instantly for many reasons, chief
among them the fact that she is really hilarious and hilar-
iously real.

Despite the gulf in years and experience, I felt comfortable sharing my story, doubts, and worries with her. I told her about my situation at work. I asked for her advice on how to deal with a difficult manager. I asked her how I should move forward, whom I should talk to, and how I should go about it.

The things I spoke with Shari about were not confidential. I had told my parents, grandparents, circle of friends, and coworkers the same things. I probably sounded like a broken record! But when I shared my experience with Shari, it was just different. She cared. She listened. She gave me the time, respect, and nonjudgmental advice that I had never received before in my life.

Shari and I got even closer when my underemployment took a turn for the worse. Many of my coworkers and I had come to a point where our low morale was affecting us outside of work. We were gaining weight, missing home, and losing perspective. Plus, our manager was completely overwhelmed and unfit for the task at hand. Her inadequacies showed in the way she acted and the comments she said to us, some of which would have made any decent HR person sweat bullets. But we were all twenty-somethings in our first real job—we thought angry and disparaging bosses were the norm.

When the comments from our manager got too out of hand, I turned to Shari. She had been helpful before in navigating office politics—she ran and still runs several of her own businesses—so I turned to her to vent and ask for advice.

She armed me with a fine list on how to talk with my manager: what to say, what not to say, what specific words I should use, and what words to avoid. The next day, I shared that list with my coworkers. They couldn't get over how practical, simple, and useful the advice was.

At one point, I turned to my coworkers and asked, "Don't you guys have people to talk to about these sorts of things?" A couple of them shrugged. One had a mom whom she talked to a lot, but only because she told her everything. For most of the others, they didn't have a single person they could turn to for direction like I did. I realized that my coworkers needed a Shari in their lives to help them navigate frustrations, dead-ends, lackluster days, and that horrible feeling of stagnation.

It occurred to me that my coworkers needed to meet Shari.

SHARI AT THE TABLE

When Meghan asked me to talk to her coworkers, I was thrilled. That's because I believe that in order to get on the right path, you first need to talk, then you need to seek the right counsel, and next, you need to "do." I was excited to help her coworkers with all three steps.

I noticed that Meghan and the others came prepared to learn with notepads and pens. I too came prepared with writing material, because I knew I would get a lot out of our meeting as well.

We sat at a table in a cozy French café on the east side of Austin. We chatted for a bit and got to know each other, but I could tell that some of them were anxious to move on to the reason why we were all there.

I knew that helping this group would be a challenge—but I was confident, because I had seen this so many times before. I have seen it in the women whom I conduct seminars for, I have seen it in my children, I have seen it in the young people whom I have employed. Whenever I talk with people who are in this situation, I feel from experience that there is only one right and necessary way to proceed. So, I opened up my body language. I sat up tall, so I could hear anyone who wanted to speak, and I put my hands on the table. To me, this is a gesture of goodwill. I wanted to signal to them that I was open, vulnerable, and receptive so that they might be too. I wanted them to feel like we were equals while sitting at that table.

I took in the faces around me, and I said, "I'm listening.

Tell me what is going on." I needed to find out the particulars of the situation. I had heard Meghan's tale of woe, but I wanted to make sure everyone was on the same page.

The floodgates opened. They told me of their workload (very light), how their manager spoke to them (passive-aggressively), what outlets they had for venting (very few), and who they reached out to for advice (outside of each other, no one). I heard a wide range of emotion in their voices, everything from frustration to hopelessness to anger. I felt bad for them, because they didn't even seem to know where their anger was directed. It seemed to me they were angry at their boss, at their company, at their friends, but mostly at themselves for letting a situation like this happen. They were all bright, talented, and inspired people, yet they had all found themselves feeling trapped.

"I go to work. I sit. I avoid my boss. She hasn't looked at me for two and a half weeks. Then I go home, and I'm too tired to do anything. Then it starts all over," one of them said. The rest nodded in approval.

"I tried talking to my mom about how I was feeling, and she cares, but she doesn't know how to help me or what to say. You know, she worked her whole life, but it was never a career. I want a career," another said.

"My boss sat me down and told me that I was too eager for

the job at hand. I'm in customer service! I thought that was what it is all about; plus, that's just who I am."

I nodded along to their stories. I found myself wincing. My heart broke for those young ladies and gentlemen. What really tore me up wasn't just the things they were saying, but the way in which they were saying them. They were depressed. They were tired. They had displaced aggression, and I could see it in their body language. I saw it in the way they leaned too far over the table and the way one of them clenched his jaw.

I wanted to yell, "It's not your fault!" But I knew there was a time and place for that, and this wasn't it!

By the time everyone had vented their frustrations, an hour and a half had passed. Like in all of my private coaching relationships and other personal and professional relationships, I felt honored that they trusted me with their stories, feelings, and emotions. I felt especially privileged because I knew that some of them couldn't or wouldn't even tell their parents, friends, or significant others this information.

That open and honest moment at the table left a significant impression on me. I realized we were doing something important by sitting and sharing at the table. We weren't complaining. To me, complaining is an act of sharing that brings you nowhere. We were getting somewhere and learning; we were communicating. We were communicating about the good, the bad, and the ugly. That is so important for a healthy life—and this was the first step on that path for these eager, willing, and able twenty-somethings.

Balance is crucial in a healthy relationship, so before I moved on to the "counsel" portion of our talk, I wanted to acknowledge their struggles by sharing struggles of my own when I was in their shoes. I shared, and I was earnest. It is important to mirror the openness of the other people at the table. It creates a feeling of mutual vulnerability that leads to respect.

I told them,

> I've been through so many different company cultures. I've seen the bosses that are cruel to you, threatened by you, or worse, ignore you. I too have been in situations where I had no one to talk to, no way to know where to turn, no one to ask what I should do. I was in a similar situation at my first "real" job, entering the corporate world in my early twenties at the height of the 1980s Wolf of Wall Street culture. Plus, I was in sales; I was a young woman in a man's world. It was unnerving. I can't believe when I hear people complain about how fun and rowdy offices used to be back in the "good old days" before human resources and laws came into

play. I believed in decorum. I believed in dignity. Yet, I was the small fish in the big office. I didn't yet know that there was a way up and out of my situation. But I took the necessary time to learn it.

Once I shared my story, I noticed the body language of the people around the table had changed. They seemed more relaxed, more confident, more validated in their feelings and experiences.

I said, "All right, everyone, get your pens out. We're now entering the counsel stage." I had them write down a to-do list, which consisted of some of the same information that I had already given Meghan. I wanted them to go and implement the strategies and then come back to me, and we would readjust accordingly.

I said, "It will be a give-and-take, and it might require some time, but we'll get you all back on your feet."

After I gave them counsel, we entered the "doing" step. I said, "Listen, I hear that there is so much more left to say on both of our ends. But we need action. We need to 'do.' Would you all like to form a group? We could get together every few weeks to talk about the action you all took." I explained that one of my passions in life was helping young people succeed. They were excited, and we all exchanged emails.

I beamed to myself as I left that restaurant that night and thought, "This is my group! I want to be there at the table for them. We're going to do great things together." It would be a challenge—but man, do I love a challenge.

But then a day passed, a week passed, a month passed, and I still had not heard from them. Not one of them reached out to me again except for Meghan. I couldn't help but be perplexed. They were ready to sit at the table. They were ready to talk. There were so many unmet needs, so many unanswered questions.

I told some of my business-owner friends about what those twenty-somethings were dealing with, and they were just as shocked as I was. We wondered how much damage their experience would do to them in the long run. They were so ready and willing to work, to get their postgraduate lives started, but they just couldn't. I felt like I could help them, but they needed to be receptive to me.

I emailed the group, again asking to meet. No response.

One night months later, as Meghan and I were sitting, catching up, on the patio of a chic place in Austin, we discussed what it was that got Meghan in that chair on a regular basis. What led Meghan out of that toxic environment and on a path upward?

Meghan came to the table week after week. She and I met at the table regularly, we shared openly, and we both benefited from it. I thought that because I got that initial group to the table, they were ready to start a partnership with me like the one I had with Meghan. But that just wasn't the case.

The difference was, our relationship had blossomed naturally. I had had no expectations.

I looked over at Meghan and said, "Your coworkers needed help, and I wanted to give it. But I wanted to give it on my own terms. They wanted the help but wanted it on their own terms. I wanted to sit at that table with them until they felt good about where they were in their lives, but they weren't ready to come back to the table yet. Just take a look at us. Do you see what we have? Our relationship is on both our own terms. We're equals.

CHAPTER 2

Generational Gap Leads to Generational Hate Leads to Generational Gap

What limited the interaction and relationship between Shari and Meghan's coworkers was what we call a "gap." The gap was not caused by Shari, nor was it caused by Meghan's coworkers.

The gap was there long before we all sat down at the table.

The gap is caused by mistrust, misinformation, and a lack of communication among generations of people for as far back as we can go. This gap prevents the sharing of information, the practice of vulnerability, and most importantly, the cross-generational partnerships that help all boats rise. This gap has been there since man had language, and it has only been growing wider since man has had access to the computer.

What is this gap, and where did it come from?

Older and younger generations have always trumpeted stereotypical criticisms of the other. At the risk of sounding melodramatic, the gap has been there since, well, the beginning. Well, maybe not, but at least we can trace it back a couple of thousand years.

In Aristotle's book *Rhetoric*, which he wrote in the fourth century BC, he complains, "[Young people] are high-minded because they have not yet been humbled by life, nor have they experienced the force of circumstances. ... They think they know everything and are always quite sure about it."

Around 20 BC, in Book III of *Odes*, Horace writes: "Our sires' age was worse than our grandsires'. We, their sons, are more worthless than they; so in our turn we shall give the world a progeny yet more corrupt." Man, Horace, lighten up!

One of our favorite examples is from an 1816 issue of

the *Times* of London in which the author laments a new overtly sexual craze that was sweeping youth culture. The lewd practice she was referring to was the waltz. "The indecent foreign dance called the Waltz was introduced... at the English Court on Friday last. ...It is quite sufficient to cast one's eyes on the voluptuous intertwining of the limbs, and close compressure of the bodies...to see that it is far indeed removed from the modest reserve which has hitherto been considered distinctive of English females. ... [Now that it is] forced on the respectable classes of society by the evil example of their superiors, we feel it a duty to warn every parent against exposing his daughter to so fatal a contagion."[1]

Yes, young adults were chastised for waltzing. Why? Because the common dancing custom at the time was that dancing partners danced side by side with minimal body contact. However, the waltz requires dance partners to face each other. Facing your dance partner was considered a "fatal contagion!"

Can you believe those vulgar youths?

The journalist, Elspeth Reeve, wrote an article in the *Atlantic* entitled "Every Every Every Generation Has Been the Me Me Me Generation" in response to Joel Stein's cover of *Time* magazine in which he claims that millennials are the "Me Me Me Generation" who are a bunch of "lazy, entitled narcissists who still live with their parents." Stein's stance is pretty brutal, but Reeve points out that nearly every generation has been accused of similar "atrocities."[2]

Reeve goes on to chronicle the long history of generational hate in America. In that article, Reeve goes back as far as a September 1907 article in which the author laments the failing of American marriages due to the "worship of the brazen calf of the self." She goes on to cite articles that appeared throughout the decades and up into the 2000s.

The funny thing is, as Reeve notes, the rhetoric around generational hate is pretty consistent from generation to generation. It seems that throughout the ages, youths—no matter the decade they are born—are always classified as self-obsessed.

Reeve cites an article in the August 1976 edition of *New York*, in which Tom Wolfe declares the 1970s as the "Me Decade." An article in the *New York Times* in 1976 said that the "youth were too busy navel gazing to care about politics...The Me Generation." In 1985, *Newsweek* ran a story called the "Video Generation", which railed against the narcissism evident in the fact that youths were using new gadgets called cameras. *Time* ran a story called "Twenty-something," which basically went into great detail about how Gen Xers were fickle, hedonistic, and void of an ability to accomplish much. In 1996, *Swing* plastered a cover story called "Generational Warfare" on the cover of their magazine.

So, we ask, who is the true entitled, lazy, narcissistic generation? Maybe all of them? Maybe none of them? Will the real entitled, lazy, narcissistic generation please stand up?

Maybe we can never know, since it would be nearly impossible to accurately judge each individual member of a generation and calculate how they measure up to those who came before them.

Our point is this: generational hate is ubiquitous. Almost always, the younger generation will be seen as lazy, provocative, entitled, and narcissistic. The older generation will always seem stuck in their ways, grouchy, judgmental, narrow-minded, and thinking that all of those things are their "rite of passage."

Now, it seems, there is one extra variable that has changed the hate dynamic. Before, the older generation held the decision-making power in the media. They could control the monologue, they could control the editorials, they could control how opinions were framed. Now, however, with the rise of technology and easy access to the internet, the younger generation has a medium (or many mediums) in which to voice their opinions and respond. And voice their opinions they do—on Facebook, Twitter, Instagram, blogs, vlogs, clogs...you name it, it's there.

Nowadays, hate can fly in both directions. Because it does, it feels as though the generational gap is wider than it's ever been. Maybe that is true, maybe it is not. But the power of the pen (or keyboard) is undeniable. If people are hearing it, writing it, and reading it, it feels real enough to be true. Whether we like it or not, rhetoric informs our subconscious (just reference the consequences of Russian ad purchases on social media platforms in the 2016 presidential election). It is hard to argue against it and hard to deny even if we want to.

THE "M" WORD

The millennial generation is now at the age where they are the target of most attacks. "Millennial," to some, has become a four-letter word defined by narcissism, entitlement, and an unwillingness to listen and learn. There are a lot of people singing that tune.

Take Simon Sinek, for example. Sinek, an author and consultant, is commonly found speaking on the subject of the generational gap. One of his more popular videos about millennials in the workplace garnered more than five million online views.

In that video, Sinek states that millennials are accused

of being "entitled and narcissistic, self-interested, unfocused, and lazy—but entitled is the big one."[3] No new information there; millennials and most every generation before them have been accused of those things. Moving on...

Next, Sinek explains with a laugh that millennials want a purpose in what they do. This jab hit home for us. Can you fault someone for wanting a purpose? Isn't finding a purpose and living for it what life's all about? Why is it laughable to him that people want to and should be able to find purpose in their work? Purpose isn't a bad thing. No one should feel guilty for pursuing a purpose.

Later on in his monologue, Sinek contradicts himself and laments how, in "the best case scenario," millennials will grow up and go through life "just never really finding joy. They'll never really find deep, deep fulfillment in work or in life; they'll just waft through life, and things will only be 'just fine.' 'How's your job?' 'It's fine, same as yesterday...' 'How's your relationship?' 'It's fine...' That's the best-case scenario."

Does he want us to find purpose, or does he not want us to find purpose?

Sinek moves on from that point and straight into the reasons millennials are still not happy.

For the sake of brevity, we will not reiterate his points—we recommend you check his videos out yourself. We can get behind some of the things Sinek says, some of the time. Yes, technology has had an impact on anyone who uses it—it is addictive, and it is designed to be addictive. That is true.

But we do not agree that you can just make a blanket statement about the emotional or psychological state of a whole generation. Sinek makes a claim that millennials are the most depressed generation, citing increased suicide rates. Although it is true that in the US the suicide rate for people from the ages of twenty to thirty-five went up from 12.2 percent to 15.5 percent from 2000 to 2015, this statistic was taken out of context. Suicide rates for every single generation (save for people eighty-five and older, who went from 19.7 percent to 19.6 percent from 2000 to 2015) went up. Suicide rates for people thirty-five to forty-four went from 14.5 percent to 17.1 percent, for people forty-five to sixty-four from 13.5 percent to 19.6 percent, and for people sixty-five to eighty-four from 14.6 percent to 16.1 percent.[4]

Suicide is a delicate topic, one that deserves to be looked at more closely.

If you look at the world and world history with a wider lens, depression, anxiety, suicide, and other dark places lurk everywhere. We all experience those feelings, but it would be unfair to say that millennials are special in that context. The increasing rate of suicide isn't just a millennial issue; it is an every-generation issue—it is unfair of him to say otherwise.

Some of what Sinek claims is hard to listen to. If you are a millennial, you might say, "Yeah, some of that sounds like me," or, "No, none of that sounds like me." This is the problem with Sinek's stance. He completely overgeneralizes a whole swath of people and distills millions of people's personalities, motivations, and actions into a handful of characteristics.

Sinek does have some valid points that are important to mention here. He says, "What this young generation needs to learn is patience. That some things that really, really matter, like love or job fulfillment, joy, love of life, self-confidence, a skill set; any of these things, all of these things, take time. Sometimes you can expedite pieces of it, but the overall journey is arduous, long, and difficult. If you don't ask for help and learn that skill set, you will fall off the mountain."

We can certainly get behind this idea that anyone—not just millennials—is eager to get going.

Up to this point, Sinek's observations are generalized, wrong, taken out of context, or a little of all three.

Overgeneralizing perpetuates stereotypes. You are not one thing; you are so many things. So is everyone else around you.

Generalization and stereotyping gets us nowhere. It leads us to racism, prejudice, and hate. It makes us homophobic, sexist, racist, and ageist.

It has led us to a place where millennial bashing seems to be on a lot of people's to-do list. We have to admit, we thought Sinek was pretty funny at first glance. But the more sweeping and baseless proclamations he made, the more we realized that his rant was just a big bucket of fuel poured over the fires that increase the generation gap. His video is an entertaining watch, for sure. But all it does is widen the chasm between "us" and "them."

At the very end of his rant, Sinek partially redeems himself when he addresses the gap. He says,

> Which is why we're taking this amazing group of young, fantastic kids who were just dealt a bad hand and it's no fault of their own, and we put them in corporate environments that care more about the numbers than they do about the kids. They care more about the short-term gains than the life of this young human being. We care more about the year than the lifetime. We are putting them in corporate environments that

are not helping them build their confidence. That aren't helping them learn the skills of cooperation. That aren't helping them overcome the challenges of a digital world and finding more balance. That isn't helping them overcome the need for instant gratification and teach them the joys and impact and the fulfillment you get from working hard on something for a long time that cannot be done in a month or even in a year. So we thrust them into corporate environments, and the worst thing is they think it's them. They blame themselves. They think it's them who can't deal. And so it makes it all worse. It's not them. It's the corporations, it's the corporate environment, it's the total lack of good leadership in our world today that is making them feel the way they do. They were dealt a bad hand, and it's the company's responsibility to pick up the slack and work extra hard and find ways to build their confidence, to teach them the social skills that they're missing out on.

He sees, in part, a cause and symptom of generational gap.

Sinek and others may have good intentions. Sinek seems to genuinely care about solving the "millennial issue." Whether or not his ideas result in success, we hope that a greater understanding of one another is a by-product.

But despite his assumed good intentions, the way he is

going about it is all wrong. He and many other thought leaders on the topic are coming at the problem with pre-conceived notions and overgeneralizations that just add more noise to the echo chamber.

STAY AWAY FROM THE LEDGE, THEY SAID

The consequences of all that noise were clear the night we sat around the table with Meghan's coworkers. We saw the residuals of the rhetoric that has widened the generational gap in the way they acted toward Shari.

They did share their frustrations with her, that is true. However, they shared because they needed to; the pressure had built up, and they needed to vent. But they didn't open up a true communication channel with her.

The fact that they didn't open up a communication channel is not their fault, though. Why would they think that was even a possibility? They could not communicate with their boss, nor their parents. They were not receiving guidance from other resources.

They saw the gap and stayed away from the ledge. They looked at Shari and asked themselves, "What makes her any different?" They came to the table with too many preconceived notions perpetuated by generation-bashing rhetoric to do any good for themselves. They didn't remember that people are more than you perceive them to be.

Shari does not subscribe to the hype of the gap. She does not believe in the messages perpetuated by millennial bashing. She is not one of a kind, though. There are many others like her; they come to the table looking to bridge the gap and make a connection.

What exactly are you afraid of?

Are you afraid of failure? Why?

—Shari: I used to be; now I'm afraid of not trying.
Who are you afraid to fail in front of the most?

—Meghan: Myself and those whom I respect.

PART II

Traditional Mentorship Is Broken

CHAPTER 3

Why We Should Come to the Table

Come to the table we must! We cannot afford to keep to ourselves. By coming to the table and bridging the gap, we allow ourselves access to the incredibly talented, experienced, storied, and accomplished network on either side of the divide.

There are people on either side of the gap who have something valuable to contribute. This is especially true for those in the older generations. You may feel, as a twenty-something, that you have experienced, seen, and learned a lot. But nine times out of ten, your age will be a limiting factor. If you plot "experience" on an X-Y graph, one of the axes will be "time." The longer you live on this earth, the more shit you'll see. Period.

The older you are, the more time you have had to gather crazy experiences, interesting stories, important life lessons, and the wisdom that comes with growth. We're not trying to inflame ageism—it's just, more often than not, the way it is.

A NOTE ON TIME FROM MEGHAN

As a kid, I was always drawn to my grandparents and their friends. They came from a different time—one that I would never know, but one that I knew I could see best if I looked back through their eyes. So, I collected their stories. I studied their faded photographs. I worshiped the collection of tiny chain-link purses my grandmother kept in a cabinet in her bathroom. The purses were so tiny—smaller than a deck of cards—and women wore them while on dates. I couldn't believe it! All they brought for a night on the town was a tube of lipstick and a compact of blush. No money, no key, no pepper spray! I can't imagine a time when young women went out at night armed only with makeup.

My grandma always laughed at my incredulous reaction to those purses. "It's just the way it was, Meggie," she would say.

She understood the world in a very different way than I did because she lived through a longer span of time than I could conceive of. She understood why things were, because she had seen where things had come from.

I kept the bits of experience my grandparents and their friends shared close to my heart because I felt that, through something like osmosis, I could absorb a tiny bit of secondhand knowledge.

It was like I could live my life armed with the wisdom of those who walked before me. It was a powerful way to live. When my grandma, who was my best friend, passed, the grief was unbearable. But I kept remembering how she dealt with the passing of her brother, mother, and Aunt Rose. She mourned with dignity and grace—and I knew that I had to do so as well.

A lot of people can't do that.

But by listening to my grandma talk about the loss of her loved ones, it prepared me for the loss of her. I surrounded myself in the community of her lifelong friends. They embraced me fully, and I leaned on them for support.

This story is a small way to say, "We gain an insane amount of wisdom and strength from those who have been through 'it' before. Whatever 'it' is, you can find someone who has been through 'it.' To tap into that reservoir of power, you have to lean across the table, bridge the divide, and create a community around you."

GET CONNECTED

We need a community—it's a fact. Professor Nicholas Christakis, MD, PhD, of Harvard University and Professor James Fowler, PhD, of the University of California San Diego jointly wrote a book called *Connected: How Your Friends' Friends' Friends Affect Everything You Feel, Think, and Do*.[1] If you've ever heard someone say, "It has been proven that your friends will make you fat," they are referring to information found in *Connected*. Both Christakis and Fowler are geniuses in their fields and make important claims based on a wealth of knowledge and research.

Their primary claim? Connectedness is everything. Connection, which they often refer to as "social network" (they are not referring to social media, but rather to a real-life social web that we all live in), is essential; it has been essential for millennia.

Human sociability and social networks have ancient genetic roots: apes form social ties, hunt in groups, maintain enduring social bonds, and derive advantages in terms of how long they live and how well they reproduce from these ties. ...The tendency to form social unions beyond reproductive ones is biologically encoded in humans: we seek out friends, not just mates. (p. 232)

The importance of connectedness is not just understood to be important at the biological level, but at the spiritual level as well. "Theologians and philosophers, like modern biologists and social scientists, have always known that social connections are key to our humanity." (p. 288)

Fowler and Christakis also discuss how powerful our networks are in shaping who we are, what we do, and what we become.

Our connections affect every aspect of our daily lives... how we feel, what we know, whom we marry, whether we fall ill, how much money we make, and whether we vote all depend on the ties that bind us. Social networks spread happiness, generosity, and love. They are always there, exerting both subtle and dramatic influence over our choices, actions, thoughts, feelings, even our desires. (p. 7)

Our connections lift us up. "Interconnection is not only a natural and necessary part of our lives but also a force for good. Just as brains can do things that no single neuron can do, so can social networks do things that no single person can do." (p. xvi)

This all sounds pretty great. But there is a caveat. Although connection is a power for good (it is proven that students with studious roommates become more studious [p. 22], having happy friends and family is a better predictor of happiness than earning more money [p. 51], and our social networks can even make us appear smarter [p. 290]), its influence can also be a power for bad. Through our connections, we can become unhealthy, sick, depressed, and unmotivated if our friends (and our friends' friends) are as well.

Our friends' friends and our friends' friends' friends have a bearing on our lives. "Our connections do not end with the people we know. Beyond our own social horizons, friends of friends of friends can start chain reactions that eventually reach us, like waves from distant lands that wash up on our shores" (p. 7). Christakis and Fowler were not joking around. That is why we need to pick our connections and our community very carefully.

There are people out in the world who know the power of our networks and have made a life of fame and fortune out of choosing wisely. Keith Ferrazzi is one of those people.

Keith Ferrazzi, an author of two seminal works on networking and community building, knows the power of a network and is a master at building them. Many people think of Keith as the expert on relationships; in fact, he is known as "Mr. Relationship." Keith gets it.

In his second book, *Who's Got Your Back*, Keith recalls his time researching his first book, *Never Eat Alone*.[2] To put together material for the book, he tapped into his "world-class" network of "clients, lawyers, bankers, vendors, or board members...for specific advice" (p. 13). Mind you, these people weren't just any clients, lawyers, vendors, and so on—they were people at the top of their industries. Keith runs with the upper echelon of thought-leaders, business executives, and movers and shakers; these people were not just your average Joes—they were experts at what they do.

Despite the fact that Mr. Relationship had a network comprised of extraordinary people, he ran into a major problem when he realized that his wide-reaching network just wasn't going to cut it. Keith explains,

> The help they could give me was relegated to a call here or a coffee there—dribs and drabs. I didn't have anyone in my life whom I could turn to at any time for a completely candid, no-holds-barred discussion of what was really going on in my life and my business. I hadn't established the kind of close, deep relationships with a few key people who would do whatever it took to make sure I never failed, and for whom I would do the same. (p. 13)

SHARI'S SIMILAR SITUATION

I was in a similar situation a few years back. The day I turned fifty, I took account of my life. I was not where I wanted to be. My life was not full of the people I needed. It was time for a redirection of my focus, not just personally, but also professionally.

I lacked a support system (in any form). Truthfully, the comrades of my past were not the people whom I would have counted on. During this transitional time, I knew that more than my address was going to have to change.

But I was smart, had a will to succeed, had desire, and was just daring enough. I saw this as a great opportunity to bring in new mentors, new like-minded individuals, and learn new lessons. After a lot of work on myself and a long search, I found my inspiration in a new network of people who wanted to make a mark. We were all about the "doing." We jumped in headfirst. I turned my life around 180 degrees and started on a dynamite adventure.

KEITH'S REALIZATION

Keith had a similar epiphany. He realized that this extensive network was full of people who would gladly sit down with him and participate in "medium talk" (a slightly more involved version of small talk), but what Keith needed was more than that. There was something missing—something he couldn't put his finger on at that time, but something that he knew existed. He had experienced it once before with his colleagues and bosses while working at the consulting firm, Deloitte & Touche. There, he had found his way into a very special community.

The community was comprised of a group of his colleagues who would spend hours talking with each other in a supportive, constructively critical, open, trusting, and respectful environment.

Keith had fallen into that group purely by accident; it wasn't something that he had sought out. Looking back, he didn't realize how important it was for his personal and professional development. The professors at the fancy business school he had gone to never once mentioned it.

He realized that he needed to find a group like that again. This time, he would make it himself.

He would model it after the group he had at Deloitte. They would be a team of people who, as Keith Ferrazzi put it in *Who's Got Your Back*, "work well together," "encourage each other," and "trust each other." A group in which everyone "raised their voices, traded their opinions, shared ideas over long slow dinners, and took lots of chances and forgave each other often." (p. 3)

In his book, Keith outlined how he did it and how his readers can copy his process.

His book is fabulous and we recommend reading it. Keep in mind that Keith has a reputation and name that precede him. He is a prodigy marketing genius who went to Harvard Business School and became the youngest CMO in Deloitte's history. By the time he wrote his book he'd had decades of experience, and his resume had afforded him a certain clout.

We wish all of us could have the chance to mine a network like his, but unfortunately, most of us do not...yet.

We don't (yet) have his Rolodex of contacts, we don't (yet) have the resume that precedes us, we don't (yet) have our faces on book covers, and we don't (yet) stand on stages to deliver speeches. What we're saying is that Keith's intentions and advice are right on, but most of us don't (yet) have the resources to put his advice into action.

But we desperately need to put his advice into action! We all need a community and a table of supporters, especially when we are young, alone, and lost!

We're here to help you find that so that one day you too can become like Keith.

CHAPTER 4

The Table

We want you to have a group who enables you to flourish like it does for Keith, Meghan, and Shari.

We will call this group your TableMates. They are the people who will come to the table and sit down with you. They will offer you advice and guidance; they will be a nonjudgmental sounding board; they will provide you with constructive criticism; they will keep your confidence; above all, they will be people whom you respect and trust and who respect and trust you.

These people will be your Board of Directors. In the driest sense, a Board of Directors is "a recognized group of people who jointly oversee the activities of an organization, which can be either a for-profit business, nonprofit organization, or a government agency."[1] In a larger sense, they act as a body that "promote[s] the success of the company for the benefit of its members as a whole."[2]

We like to think of your TableMates as your Board of Directors. They are there to help oversee your activities and work to enable your success.

In *Who's Got Your Back*, Keith says that it takes three people who will help change your life, but to us, the number doesn't matter.

Meghan has eight TableMates at the time of publication. At different times in her life, she has had a lot more and a lot less. All of them have come to her table from different walks of life and from different parts of her network. She met one through her job, others through family, some through friends, and others by chance. They range in age from twenty-five to almost eighty. Although each of them help her in all areas of her life, she turns to specific TableMates for specific situations to participate in TableTalk. Something wrong at work? She turns to Shari. Something going on with her mom or her boyfriend? She turns to Scott. When she wants to talk about spirituality, psychology, and all things having to do with the soul, she schedules a dinner with Sheila. When she needs a kick in the ass to get herself going on a project that she has been putting off, she turns to her short list of three go-getters.

It would be so silly of Meghan to limit how many Table-Mates sit at her table. Her mom taught her "the more the merrier." When it comes to your table, this rings true. There are some exceptions, however, that must be addressed. As Christakis and Fowler warn, contagion is real. We don't want to poison your group by bringing in someone toxic. We will explore how to filter in a later chapter.

MEGHAN ON HER TABLEMATES

The number of people who surround you and act as your Board of Directors simply depends on your individual needs and wants. Some people have two; others have dozens. Once you start on this journey of bringing people to your table, there will always be an ebb and flow. People will cycle out; your group will grow or shrink. But once you see the benefits of keeping TableMates, you will want to keep your table full.

When I need guidance, a shoulder to cry on, an ear to listen to, a fire lit under me, or a story to remind me that all bad things come to an end, I can turn to one or all of my TableMates. The beautiful thing is that they also turn to me. We provide mutual resilience and perspective within a trusting and respectful environment. The good flows both ways.

Shari is one of my TableMates. It became clear to me the

night I took her to talk with my coworkers. That night, I realized she wasn't just a client, she wasn't just a friend, she wasn't just a kind adult who had stumbled into my life—she was so much more. I didn't have the word for it then, but our relationship was something different, something unique. It was not one that I had sought out. It was not one that I tried to force. I had had professional mentors before, but this was more of a holistic sort of mentorship: professional and personal, real-life and relatable.

SHARI'S TAKE ON TABLEMATES

Meghan and I connected during a period of intense growth and change in both of our lives. I was stepping out of my career and starting a new one. Meghan was beginning her career after a couple of years of feeling stuck and lost.

We first met through work. I was a partner in a private telecommunications company and own several other businesses, so I wanted to consolidate what I had learned about sales and customer service into a book. I scared the shit out of myself, because although I wanted to write a book more than anything, it is a seriously intimidating endeavor. I was anxious, sure, but I knew it was the right next step for me. Yes, it was going to be a challenge. But to me, "challenge" is not a negative word: it's a place to start. If I tried and it didn't work out, that's okay—at least I tried!

A TableMate of mine who was also writing a book recommended a company that could help me get my words on a page. So, I reached out to them, and they connected me with a young woman—Meghan. She was introduced to me as my "editor." Put yourself in my shoes for a moment. I want to start a new career; I want to consolidate decades of success into a book, and Meghan, who was twenty-four years old at the time, is supposedly going to get me there.

Many people would shake their heads and say, "You're putting your future success into the hands of a twenty-something?" They couldn't believe it. But I would just shrug, and say, "So what? She can do the job; why does it matter?" I didn't see her age. Certainly, I wasn't going to dismiss her before I even knew her.

I approached our first meeting with that mindset. And although I was nervous, Meghan instantly put me at ease. She gave me confidence. I liked the way she spoke and her calming and open demeanor. The way she handled herself made me feel like I could respect and connect with her, and that made me have the utmost trust in her. She also had so much experience that I didn't have, and I was open to following her lead. She believed in what I had to say and worked through the material with me, which brought us together through mutual trust.

After only a couple of meetings, I realized that I actually

enjoyed how Meghan was of a different generation. I mean, I was writing that book with young people in mind. She brought a new perspective to the project. She suggested topics and asked questions that I hadn't even considered.

For instance, when we were putting together the chapter on how to manage a team, we had a long discussion about relationships between managers and their employees. We both believe that hierarchy has changed within companies. During my time in the corporate world, your boss was your boss; he was not your friend. There was a strict line that you did not cross. Now, though, we think those lines are becoming thinner and disappearing altogether in some cases. Meghan pushed me to address that changing atmosphere and to think hard about the changing landscape of work relationships.

After Meghan and I worked together for a couple of months, a box arrived at my house. It was a box full of copies of my completed book.

A familiar feeling bubbled up in me again—it was the crazy fear that had been assuaged by Meghan and my publisher throughout the process. Looking at the open boxes of books, I said aloud to my son, "Oh, my god, what have I begun?"

What if no one likes them? What if these aren't any good?

My son looked at me with big eyes and said, "Well, it's a little late for that now, isn't it? Shouldn't you have thought about that a long time ago?"

I laughed, hugged him, and said, "You're absolutely right. What the hell is wrong with me? I love this. This project has been so great."

My fear was healthy, but unfounded. I realized that what Meghan and I had done was create a piece of art. Not in the hoity-toity sense, but in the sense that you truly have to be vulnerable. I once heard a dear friend define an artist as someone who lays himself open to the world and puts his whole self out there for everyone to judge. In doing so, he gives the world the opportunity to openly reject or accept him.

But sitting across from Meghan at that table, working on that project together, made me feel like I could trust her to help me be open to judgment and vulnerability.

Throughout the whole process of working with Meghan, I kept thinking, "Man, she is cool. I wish we could hang out." I respected her and saw her as an equal because of—not despite—the fact that she was young. She had the expertise I didn't have. But she did have the point of view and attitude I had. It was perfect!

I happened to lease a vacation house in the same city

where Meghan lived, and I was planning on heading down there for a weekend. So, I casually asked if she wanted to meet. She agreed to meet, and the rest is history.

Our relationship has brought so much to my life. Neither of us stop learning. Neither of us want to stop talking. We advise each other and work through our losses together. We get so excited to sit across the table from one another.

There is no hierarchy, there is a mutual respect, and there is a lot of adventure!

MORE THAN A MENTOR

Shari came to the table without pretense. She never approached her relationship with Meghan like she knew the answer to everything. She never acted holier than thou. She never sat on her high chair and lorded over Meghan. She came with a learner's mind.

This is an important lesson because TableMates should come to the table with a learner's mind just like Shari did.

Everyone needs TableMates; everyone needs a handful of Shari's. Some people are out there trying to find them, but so many people simply go about it in the wrong way: they're mistakenly looking for a mentor.

Shari is not a mentor. She is a TableMate. TableMates do mentor, but they are so much more than a mentor.

Tim Ferriss, in his book *Tribe of Mentors*, lauds the advice of the dozens of mentors who contributed to his book. Tim touts them as mentors, but to us they are no more than gods placed on a pedestal. These people are heroes, but they aren't necessarily the people who will help bring you along on your journey. The advice they lend is spoken *at everyone*, not *to you*.

There is a difference.

At everyone is not enough. Taking an individual's unique experience and broadly applying his or her advice to a wide swath of people, we feel, is gravely insufficient. If that is what smart people like Tim Ferriss are calling "mentoring," then we should be looking beyond mentors.

We should be looking for TableMates.

A TableMate is a person who is *physically there*, who *knows you*, and who has *time for you*.

CHAPTER 5

The Shoulder

Traditional mentorships are broken.

Consider this fictionalized case study from Harvard Business School entitled "Can Nice Guys Finish First?" by Jeffrey Pfeffer.[1]

The case follows Adam, an intelligent, well educated, and experienced young COO of Straus Event Specialists. Adam finds himself in a predicament with Merwyn Straus, the CEO of the company. Adam discovered and calculated the risks of a new venture. He presented his findings to Merwyn, and they both agreed that they should move forward with the venture because it seemed to be very lucrative. Adam wanted to be placed as the CEO of the venture. But Merwyn denied his request. "The door is closed," he told Adam. Adam could not understand

Merwyn's decision and so tried to reason with him, but Merwyn wouldn't budge.

Up until that point, Adam practically worshiped Merwyn. Adam wondered how to "begin to explain the depth of his respect and admiration for Merwyn, who was teaching him everything there was to know about the event-planning business—and who constantly sang Adam's praises and promoted his career." But, everything had changed in the course of a conversation.

In the story, one of Adam's friends, Sarah, hears about how Merwyn shot Adam down. After hearing what Merwyn said to Adam, Sara says, "That is the most condescending, infantilizing thing I ever heard."

This case study is meant to induce conversation among students at Harvard Business School. Should Adam stay and let his negative feelings toward Merwyn fester? Or should he leave because the mentorship seems to have been fundamentally broken?

Marshall Goldsmith, a leading executive educator and coach, presented his opinion to Harvard students. He believes that the mentorship is broken; Adam should pack his bags and head out—he has nothing more to gain from the relationship.

Adam doesn't understand that whatever mentorship he

thought he had with Merwyn no longer exists. Perhaps, at times, there were good parts to it. But that was in the past. Merwyn has ruined the mentor/mentee relationship. Merwyn has, in fact, raised what we call the "Shoulder."

THE SHOULDER

We've all heard of the term "cold shoulder."

We usually use the term when describing a situation where someone ignored you or wouldn't talk to you. We all went to middle school—we know the situation. It has also "been used as a description of aloofness and disdain, a contemptuous look over one's shoulder, and even in the context of a woman attempting to decline the advances of an aggressive man. Overall, it remains widely popular as a phrase for describing the act of ignoring someone or something, or giving an unfriendly response."[2]

If you've ever been given the cold shoulder, you know how brutal it can be. If you are a giver of the cold shoulder, power to you, but also don't be surprised when you start losing friends.

The Shoulder that we speak of is similar to a cold shoulder; however, the Shoulder involves another brutal strategic device: it is what we give to people when we want them to know that we look down upon them. When we feel or desire to be superior to someone, we give them the Shoulder. When we want to block them from being fully in our lives, we put up the Shoulder. Quite frankly, we put up that Shoulder to hide the fear of not knowing how to ask the question, or not knowing the answer, for fear of showing ignorance. This applies to both generations and becomes an inhibitor to reaching for, or receiving, help. (Seeking help is not a weakness, people.)

The Shoulder, at its core, establishes a hierarchy. It enforces an imbalance in a relationship. He who gives the Shoulder to another is basically saying, "I'm better than you; I'm above you."

Merwyn gave Adam the Shoulder. For that reason, is Merwyn likely to be a TableMate of Adam's? People who give the Shoulder cannot sit at the table, because when we're at the table, we all sit at the same level.

SHOULDER ON BOTH SIDES

You might be thinking that the only people who can give the Shoulder are older, more experienced people—people whom you would place on the mentor side of the table. But the Shoulder can actually come from both sides of the generational gap.

Remember our dear friend Stella? We met with her

because we wanted to help her. Our goal was to work with her to get to a point in her professional and social life where she felt she wasn't stuck. Our first order of business was helping her find a TableMate.

But first, we needed to get some basic information out of her. We asked her what industry or role she was passionate about. She had never previously mentioned to us what she wanted to do with her life, so we needed to start there.

For some, this question is the most difficult to answer. But Stella barely missed a beat. She confessed to us that she really wanted to work in the music industry. She wanted to do public relations for up-and-coming bands.

"Great!" we thought. "Now, all we have to do is strategize on where to start pursuing TableMates who operate in and around that industry."

"Oh, I already know someone," Stella said. "She is a big promoter."

It was too good to be true. "Why haven't you reached out to her?" we wondered.

"I just never thought I could do it," Stella said.

"You can!" we said.

Stella reached out to the woman, and they set a date to meet the very next week. Stella had never done this before, so we sat with her to prepare. We talked about some questions that she could ask her. I always like to know how that person got where they were. So, I made sure she asked the woman about her journey. After we prepped, we sent Stella on her way.

After the meeting, Stella called us. She was nearly in tears.

"What happened?" we asked.

"She didn't offer me a job," Stella said. Her voice was full of shame.

We didn't understand what she was talking about. The three of us had never spoken about Stella expecting a job out of this. We asked Stella to clarify by telling us about the whole interaction.

In a gist, the meeting went great. The two women loved the same music, the same bands, and even cringed when they learned they had the same Backstreet Boys posters in their respective rooms years ago. "But then," Stella said, "she said it was great to meet me and to call again if I wanted to meet up again."

To us, that was a total win. That's a great outcome to getting to know a potential TableMate. But Stella thought it was a disaster. We realized Stella didn't understand what we were trying to help her do.

She had come into the situation with visions of a transactional, utilitarian type of mentor relationship. She thought it worked like this: Stella reaches out, mentor takes the bait and offers job, and everyone lives happily ever after. Stella went to the table with her Shoulder up. She believed she was elevated enough in esteem that she would just be able to simply look down at the woman across the table and expect a job. She had visions of being held aloft on a throne and led toward the golden gates of employment. She wished for the hierarchy and played the hierarchy game, and when it wasn't there, she was so upset when her plan failed.

MEGHAN'S FORMAL MENTORSHIP AND THE SHOULDER

I was introduced to the idea of formal mentorship during my years in college. I had never really had extraordinary relationships with adults outside of my immediate family, but I decided that since all of my classmates were seeking mentors, I should as well. I was excited for the prospect of having someone older and wiser to guide me.

A lot of my college friends were getting mentors through

formal mentorship programs at the companies they interned at. Others found mentors through their clubs, fraternities, or classes. I ended up with a mentor whom I met outside of school.

Boy, our experiences were completely different from my experience with Shari!

The mentorships we had were formal, formulaic, businesslike. Our mentors, although generous with their time despite their very busy lives, had little time to spare outside of our monthly lunch meetings. They didn't have time for slow dinners or long phone calls. They didn't have time for us to get to know each other.

The main thing was, though, that our mentorships were built upon a steep grade. The mentors were atop the pedestal and the mentees down below. Of course, we're not equals in experience, success, and productivity. That was a given. But we were also not equals in trust, respect, and in our proclivity to have a learner's mind. The Shoulders were up.

It was a one-way road. I was the learner, the listener, the leach. They were the learned, the listened-to, and the host.

It's not that I regret those mentorships in any way. I really admire and am very thankful to the people who helped me during those times. One particular mentor, although we met infrequently, connected me to some incredible internship opportunities for which I am very grateful.

However, there was just something missing. I had the mentor, but I didn't have a connection I wanted. I was awkward and not my true self, I tried way too hard, and I was constantly worried about offending my mentor in some way. I worried that I wasn't smart enough, deserving enough, or just plain good enough. Because I didn't have an open and honest relationship where I felt free to talk openly with my mentors, those worries and doubts stayed inside and silently wreaked havoc. How could I be myself and therefore be truly open to understanding what I was learning?

I turned to some of my classmates and friends at the time. I asked them about their relationships with their mentors. They also told me similar things: they weren't connecting; they felt like their relationships were forced, formulaic; and some of them felt like they were just a waste of their mentors' time and energy. We all felt like we couldn't offer any value to our mentors.

Yes, we loved our mentors; yes, we were thankful for them; but there was something missing.

The relationship was all take and no give, and, as Adam Grant says, the best relationships need a give and a take.

EGGS IN A BASKET

Formal mentorships are designed to pursue one person. The mentee ends up throwing all of his effort and time into connecting with that one person.

In doing this, they hurt themselves. By avoiding other avenues for mentorship, they block off access to community wisdom and the support a community can offer.

They also take a risk. What if, after committing yourself to your one mentor, you come to realize that the two of you just are incompatible? Dr. Meg Jay, the author of *The Defining Decade*, calls this *lock-in*: "Lock-in is the decreased likelihood to search for, or change to, another option once an investment in something has been made."[3] This is certainly how Adam feels in his relationship with Merwyn. Where else can he go? He's put all of his eggs in Merwyn's basket, and now Merwyn has turned on him. Adam has met a dead-end, and there is nowhere to go from there.

By putting all of your eggs in one basket, you are opening yourself up to a lot of unnecessary pressure to make it work out.

We need to get away from that type of black-and-white, deal-or-no-deal type of thinking. We need to expand ourselves. We need to hedge our bets by investing in more than one person.

Spreading your search for mentorship away from just one person will also allow you access to many different people who specialize in different things and thus can offer valuable advice from new perspectives.

HAVE TO JIVE

In a sense, finding mentors is like dating. You have to meet a lot of people in order to see whom you jive with. In order to figure out if you jive, you have to get real with yourself and with the person across the table from you.

As Meghan was with her former mentors, so many people are embarrassed of "getting real" with their mentors. They feel uncomfortable with opening up and letting go. But to be a true TableMate requires honesty and openness.

When Meghan first began searching for guidance in the form of a TableMate, she had to learn how to be vulnerable. She had to learn how to say, "I'm sorry, I don't understand that," or "I'm having a really tough go of that." It took a while to learn this, but if you have the right people at your table, they won't judge you. Instead, they will encourage you and help you learn.

ASKING FOR HELP IS NOT WEAK

In contrast to Stella's ease with asking for help, Sam was reluctant to ask for help.

Sam is not alone. A lot of people have difficulties with asking for help. They mistakenly believe that doing so is weak. We think that underneath that hesitation is a fear of rejection. Those people fear reaching their hand across the table because they are afraid no one will reach out and take it.

Rejection, be it romantic, professional, personal, or otherwise, is one of the most difficult feelings to deal with. Through practice, some of us learn to cope better with it than others. But no matter what, that familiar pain of rejection is something we all know. When you sit at the table and open up and reach across the divide, you are opening yourself up to the potential for rejection.

We think another big reason people don't ask for help is that they fear judgment. No one likes to be judged. We don't like hearing that we are not on the right track, that we are behind, that we are being lazy. But, boy, sometimes we need it. Being told to get your shit together is never a fun conversation, but if presented in the right way and from someone whom you respect, it can completely correct the trajectory of your life.

THE RIGHT PEOPLE

All of these problems with mentorship can be avoided if only you find yourself at a table with the right Table-Mates. The right group will allow you to open yourself up, will establish a give-and-take, and will deliver constructive criticism with their Shoulders down and with their hearts open.

Finding those people can be scary. Reaching your hand out across the divide and hoping someone takes it is nerve-racking. But if you find the right people, you can be guaranteed that they will sit down at the table and take your hand.

CHAPTER 6

The Right People at the Table

This chapter is about finding your Board of Directors. We will go into more detail about what that means later, but first, we want to talk about getting over the fear of approaching people.

MEGHAN'S FRIEND AND FEAR OF THE BOARD

I have a friend who is a talented computer programmer. He is charming, smiley, and curious. A while ago, we were at a holiday party. He and I were some of the only guests in attendance who were in our early twenties. Most of the hundred or so other partygoers were in their forties, fifties, sixties, and seventies.

My friend seemed to be a little uneasy; he wasn't talking to too many people. That was unlike him. He was normally fearless. I've seen him do what most guys his age shake in their boots even thinking about: going up to a random girl and asking her out. He also manages to do it in a noncreepy way—it's really impressive.

Because his behavior at the Christmas party was so odd, I asked him, "What's wrong?"

He said, "I can't talk to any of these people. I just feel so dumb compared to them."

I was pretty astonished, especially considering I thought of him as one of the smartest people I knew, and likely one of the most intelligent people in the room. He was also a myriad of other great things. So why did he feel he couldn't talk to the people around him?

I understood his fear, though. I also felt it when I first started on my journey to finding TableMates.

I said, "Dude, that's not true. Even if it was, it doesn't matter. These people are just like any other person. Yes, they're older, but what difference should it make? They all experience the same emotions, setbacks, and fears. It's not a big deal—you can do this."

"It's hard for me to go up to them. But I want to because I know I want to start meeting people like them and becoming a sort of mentee."

"I get it. I also used to have major difficulty inserting myself."

"How did you get over it?" he asked.

"A lot of practice, some reading, and some tricks I learned along the way," I said.

"Like what?"

"Okay, this may sound odd, but stick with me, because it works."

I explained to him that when we think of people whom we want as our mentors, we often see them in an exaggerated light. We see all their power, influence, experience, and wisdom, and we put them on a pedestal.

But we need to refocus our perceptions. Instead of blowing these people out of proportion, and making them more intimidating than they should be, we need to humanize them. In order to do this, I suggested using a trick I discovered when I first started on my path toward gaining TableMates. Whenever I got intimidated by certain individuals, I would play a mind game with myself. I would ask myself, "What is his or her favorite dessert?" As I walked up to that person, I would assess them based on what they looked like, and what I assumed their personality was. I would assign them their favorite dessert. Then, I would picture them eating that dessert.

It's a lot less fun than picturing your audience in their underwear. But for me, it's a lot more helpful. Why do I do this? Think about it. Why do cultures across the globe bond over a shared meal? Why do business people trying to clinch a deal gather over lunches and dinners? Why do we take our dates out to a romantic restaurant? Because eating is an act of intimacy and vulnerability and that bonds us.

The act of sharing a meal goes back to caveman times when one always had to be on alert. Our early ancestors found a hack. Eat in a group, and those around you can alert you to danger when you're knuckle deep in a mammoth rib. Back then, sharing a meal with someone meant you could be vulnerable around them because you trusted them to save you. Millennia later, we gather to eat because it bonds us in a biological way. It is one of the most basic things we do as humans.

So, I make a point of picturing whoever is intimidating me eating something they love. In my mind's eye, they are happy and vulnerable, and that immediately humanizes them.

I know this sounds a little weird, but when I decided I needed to find TableMates, I was in a very bad place. While in college, my social anxiety peaked. I couldn't raise my hand in class. My grades suffered. My relationships suffered. I didn't like where I was, and I needed to do something.

I signed up for a public-speaking class with a highly regarded professor, Professor Roeglin. She helped jumpstart my journey. From there, I took improv classes and made a habit of striking up conversations with random people. I even started cold-calling people under the guise of asking for help for research papers. Over the next couple of years, I slowly got better.

A short story that I came across really impacted me on my journey, and I want to share it with anyone else who is struggling with social anxiety and confidence. It is called "The Egg" by Andy Weir.[1] The story is a conversation between a man who just died in a car accident and God. The man asks what will happen to him next, and God says that he will be reincarnated into a Chinese peasant girl in 540 AD. The dialogue is clipped for brevity, but the message remains intact.

"Wait, what?" the man said. "You're sending me back in time?"

The God figure tells him technically, "yes." The man considers God's answer and asks, "What was the point of it all?"

The rest of the story, told from God's perspective, goes as so:

"Seriously?" I asked. "Seriously? You're asking me for the meaning of life? Isn't that a little stereotypical?"

"Well, it's a reasonable question," you persisted.

I looked you in the eye. "The meaning of life, the reason I made this whole universe, is for you to mature."

"You mean mankind? You want us to mature?"

"No, just you. I made this whole universe for you. With each new life, you grow and mature and become a larger and greater intellect."

"Just me? What about everyone else?"

"There is no one else," I said. "In this universe, there's just you and me."

You stared blankly at me. "But all the people on earth..."

"All you. Different incarnations of you."

"I'm every human being who ever lived?"

"Or who will ever live, yes."

"Every time you victimized someone," I said, "you were victimizing yourself. Every act of kindness you've done, you've done to yourself. Every happy and sad moment ever experienced by any human was, or will be, experienced by you."

That story fundamentally transformed how I approached people. It had nothing to do with religion or reincarnation, but rather, it just really hit home that no matter how successful, important, or intelligent the person across the table is, they are just a person stumbling through life, also unsure of its meaning. On a fundamental level, we are very much all the same.

When I started approaching people from that angle, all of my feelings of social anxiety and self-consciousness dulled. Of course, the anxiety is still there, but every year it gets quieter and quieter because I work on it. It has so little power over me now.

CONNECT WITH THE RIGHT ONES

Meghan, her friend, and many others feel like they cannot connect. We recommend learning techniques like the ones above to improve confidence in social settings.

There is one caveat. If you have practiced and have given your best to connecting with someone whom you want to bring to your table, and they are still aloof, then maybe that person is just not someone whom you should be talking to.

Whatever step you are in in your relationship with that person—whether you are at your first conversation or your fiftieth conversation—if you feel that the trust and respect is not there, then let go. That person was not right for you. You were not right for them. Don't take it too personally. Move on but move on right away. If you don't, the feelings of rejection might fester.

It's no wonder that many young people don't feel comfortable in a room filled with adults. There is just so much judgment from some people. So much ego.

Avoid those people; there are fewer of them than you would expect. Start a relationship with the right people. They will be impressed with your confidence in approaching them. That is the prize—to be able to stand tall, look someone in the eye, and gain mutual respect.

SAM AND WHO IS RIGHT

One day about a year into his job, Sam came home from work, sat on the couch, dug into a bag of chips, and opened up his Facebook app. He had had a birthday celebration the weekend before, and he noticed that a couple of people had posted pictures from the night. He clicked on one of the pictures he had been tagged in and stared at the picture for a couple of seconds. Why had his friend tagged him in the picture? He wasn't in this one. He scanned the faces again and, out loud, he groaned. He was indeed in the picture. He hadn't realized it at first because he didn't recognize himself. His face was puffy, his eyes were dull, and his smile was dim; he had gained about twenty pounds. This was a major reality check for him.

He was miserable and stuck in a cycle of bad habits that he didn't even realize he had picked up. All of them spurned from the fact that he spent ten hours a day in a job he hated with no upward movement in sight.

He called us the next day.

"You were right," he said. "I need help. I need a network. I need support. What type of person should I be looking for?"

"We need to get you a TableMate," Shari said. "But before we go on that journey, we need to explain what a Table-Mate is."

NOT NECESSARILY

How do we define a TableMate?

First, we're going to tell you what a TableMate is not necessarily. Notice we aren't using the term "not;" we are using the term "not necessarily." We are doing that because finding TableMates is not a binary process where they are either "good" or "bad." However, it is good to have guardrails to help guide us to success. The guardrails are rules, and as with any rules, there are exceptions. We are taking those exceptions into consideration, because we don't want you to overlook a great TableMate just because they fall into the following list.

A TableMate is not necessarily someone who has your ideal job. You don't need to find a TableMate who is a senior or executive in whatever industry or company you are pursuing.

A TableMate is not necessarily someone who is the picture of your ideal life.

A TableMate is not necessarily someone who is uber-successful. Basing your ideal TableMate on said TableMate's status in life is not a good way of going about your search. It's not about what your TableMate has. It's about who your TableMate is.

A TableMate is not necessarily someone who is older

than you are. Peer mentors can be just as effective even if they're technically on or below your level of experience or success. They've likely had parallel experiences and can understand what you're going through and can share their own perspectives. Don't discount how valuable that can be.

A TableMate is not necessarily someone who is wealthy. That being said, there is absolutely no harm in opening up a relationship with someone who has a big job or a big house. Sometimes, those things come with the package. We aren't recommending that you avoid those people on principle.

A TableMate is not necessarily someone who has the same goals as you. We aren't recommending that you point your search at TableMates with the same desires in life as you. For instance, you may want to be filthy rich, but your TableMate doesn't have to be, nor does she have to desire to be filthy rich. It's more about having the same morals. More on that later.

A TableMate is not necessarily someone who is similar to you. You shouldn't be looking for a "you." Condoleezza Rice, director of the Global Center for Business and the Economy at Stanford University's Graduate School of Business, and former US Secretary of State, once said, "Search for role models you can look up to and people who take an interest in your career. But here's an important warning: You don't have to have mentors who look like you. Had I been waiting for a black, female Soviet specialist mentor, I would still be waiting. Most of my mentors have been old white men, because they were the ones who dominated my field."[2]

THE RIGHT PEOPLE

Now that we've told you what a TableMate is not, let's talk about what a TableMate is. Picture the table at which you will sit with your TableMate. Consider the legs of the table. What function do those legs serve? For one, they hold the table up. They ensure that the table is solid and can support weight and stress. They guarantee that the table stays level. The characteristics of your ideal TableMate will act like the legs of the table. The better that TableMate fits the following characteristics, the sturdier your relationship infrastructure will be.

SOMEONE YOU TRUST

Trust is the first of our table legs. Trust is absolutely crucial in any relationship, but it is especially important among those who sit at the table. Consider the nature of the conversation at the table. We hope if you've found the right people that you will be talking about your innermost desires, dreams, insecurities, and failures.

We want to point out a potential trap you may encounter

in this category. We often trust our family members and the people who are closest to us. Often, they are the first people we invite to our table. This could be a good thing or a bad thing.

It can be a good thing because often the people closest to us see us more clearly than we see ourselves. They have a perspective on you that you don't have. We're sure most people have had an experience where they deliberated on a decision for a long time, and when they finally asked someone close to them what they should do, that person's answer was so obviously the right one. We get so inside our own heads that we can't see anything else.

However, there is also a downside to bringing our family and close friends to the table. Sometimes the people whom you trust and who are close to you mistake their ideas for what is best for you with what is best for them. Shari sees this all the time in the workshop she runs for people ranging in age from eighteen to thirty. On a regular basis, the mothers of the participants ask if they can come to the group sessions. Shari always tells them "no." It might sound a little harsh, but she has a good reason for it.

Shari has found that when she used to let family members into the workshops, more times than not, they would inappropriately insert themselves into the conversation. Shari remembers one time during a career brainstorming exercise, a mother of one of the participants raised her hand and said, "You know, I've always thought my daughter should be a vet or a lawyer." Shari looked over at her daughter who was shaking her head and mouthing, "No way."

People close to us have an idea of our future that eclipses ours and brings the process of planning to a complete halt. They don't do it maliciously, but their efforts are meant to be manipulative.

How terrible do you feel when your father wants you to be a consultant, but you want to do video marketing?

How guilty do you feel when you decide you don't want to have kids, but your mother can't accept that fact?

How bad is it when you want to move to a new place for a year just to try it out, but your best friend or boyfriend won't be able to handle long distance?

There are some people whom we trust, but because of their own explicit or implicit self-interest, they shouldn't be invited to your table.

SOMEONE WHO SPEAKS THE TRUTH

There are no concrete, final answers in life. Life is a mystery to all who live it. A good TableMate doesn't pretend to know the answers, but he does want to share with you his truth.

SOMEONE YOU SHARE MUTUAL RESPECT WITH

You have to be able to respect your TableMates. Conversely, they have to respect you. This is often a difficult thing to accomplish as it takes time to both gain and dole out respect. Respect is crucial because it enables you to see eye to eye, even when you disagree.

To determine if someone is deserving of respect, study their actions, and to a lesser degree, the things he or she says. Does your potential TableMate neglect his responsibilities? Does he listen to other's opinions? Does he shut down people whom he disagrees with? Does he have a track record of honesty? Does he treat others with respect?

Conversely, ask yourself if you are deserving of the respect of your TableMates. If you fear you do not, we have a conversation about improving yourself in the following chapters.

A friend of ours has a TableMate who is a respected engineer. This man—we'll call him Phillip—told us about a recent interaction he had with an engineer who wanted help licensing a new device she had patented.

Phillip met with the inventor, and they spoke for an hour—which, for Phillip, was a long meeting considering his jam-packed schedule. He thought the inventor's idea was great, and he asked her to do some homework before their next meeting. He requested she send him some more information and look up a couple of data points they would need moving forward. She happily agreed and thanked him for his help. The meeting couldn't have gone better for the inventor. He was a successful and reputable veteran in an industry she was trying to break into, and he was enthusiastic about assisting her. They set a date to meet again a week later.

The inventor never sent over the information Phillip had requested. When they met again, Phillip asked her if she had done the quick research he wanted, and again, she had failed to perform. All she came to the meeting with were excuses.

For Phillip that was the end of the mentorship because he had lost respect for the inventor. He was willing to give his time and expertise, but she wasn't willing to give him her time or energy.

The inventor unknowingly did the two things that put you on the fast track to losing respect. She didn't listen, and she didn't act.

If you listen and act, you can gain immediate respect

from your TableMate right from the get-go. Listen to your TableMate's opinions, questions, and stories. Think about how they apply to you. Tell her, "Hey, you said something interesting at our last meeting. You asked an interesting question. I've been thinking about it ever since." Even if you can't answer the question, even if you don't have some fabulous comment or insight, it doesn't matter. The fact that you listened and thought and remembered speaks volumes.

Next, act. If your TableMate asks you to do something, whether it is to read an article, email a contact she gives you, or watch a documentary, do it. It doesn't take long, it is educational, and it's for your benefit.

You'd be surprised at how few people actually do what they say they will. Stand out. Be that small percentage who does. Even if you don't get a single thing out of it, it shows dedication to the relationship. It shows that you respect your TableMate's opinion. In turn, you will get respect.

SOMEONE WHO HAS BEEN THROUGH IT BEFORE

"It" can mean whatever you want it to mean. It all depends on who or what you are looking for in a TableMate.

For instance, Meghan has a friend whose only desire in his professional life is to be an entrepreneur. If you take account of the people around his table, you will notice that a large majority are all entrepreneurs. Collectively, they have had dozens of successful ventures and dozens of failed ventures. Meghan's friend revels in the stories his TableMates tell, takes note of the hurdles they overcome, and documents the solutions they find. He loves to be around those people because one day, when he has a company of his own, he wants to have a bank of knowledge to draw from. He wants to learn from others who failed and succeeded before him. Because of the conversations he has with his TableMates, he has such a crazy amount of knowledge about small businesses that you would think he's owned a hundred of them.

He recently has taken the first steps to start a business, and he has found great comfort in his TableMates because they've been through "it" before.

This is just one example of what "it" is. But "it" can be a million different things. "It" can be a divorce that left you shaken, a difficult PhD program, a mental illness you are personally dealing with, or a spiritual journey that you want a network to help you through.

SOMEONE WHO LIVES LIKE YOU

We want you to find someone who lives life (or a part of it) like you do.

Do you want to be a fantastic dad? Find someone who is. Do you want to be someone who is known for always telling the truth? Find someone who shines in her integrity. Do you want to have a network of people who are high ranking in the business world? Find someone who strives to be uber-connected to all the "right" people.

These different traits like "honest," "dedicated," or "well connected," all contribute to your identity capital. Your identity capital is what makes you *you* and what you feel contributes to your worth.

Find people who have similar identity capital as you either already do or want to have.

SOMEONE WHO IS A LIFELONG LEARNER AND CAN LEARN FROM YOU

This is huge. We should all be lifelong learners, but often, as we age, we get set in our ways and forget how important being open to new ideas is.

Often, we hear about people who have grandparents or parents who are still very racist or sexist for no other reason than because they've always been racist or sexist.

As we settle into life, we settle. We stop growing and learning to our great detriment.

So, when looking for a TableMate, it is so important that he or she is a lifelong learner. She doesn't have to be "hip with the times," nor does he have to necessarily agree with the common sentiments of the times; but they've got to at least be open to understanding what and why society is what it is.

When someone is a lifelong learner, she or he comes to the table with a cocked ear and an open mind. He or she comes ready to learn and to share. He or she won't judge you for not knowing. Because they are perennial students, they know that the willingness to know is far more important than actually knowing.

Many people do not approach life as a learner. Many feel as if they've gone through it, they've given their time, and they don't need any more direction. Others may keep themselves naive because of fear. They fear novelty, they fear losing control of what they know, and they fear the future.

They're afraid they'll become washed out, so they claim that they know everything. But this exact process is what really makes you irrelevant. Ask any successful CEO how they stay successful, and they'll tell you it's because they are constantly on the lookout for how the world is going to change, and they prepare for it. They don't know everything, and they approach life that way.

SOMEONE WHO FILLS A SEAT

A TableMate should fulfill a specific need in you. If you just want to hang out with any ol' person, go hang out with your friends. The table is more than just a hangout place. Don't get us wrong, if you do it right, eventually your time at the table will feel like you are just hanging out with friends, but it is also a serious place where you get serious shit done.

Yes, be open to people who want to come to the table, but also have a filter that filters out people who will waste your time. Pay attention, observe, listen. Be wary. There are plenty of people who will ingratiate themselves with you for a myriad of unproductive reasons.

Sometimes, you might get a person whose only contribution is the knot in your stomach. You know those types. Keep those people out, because not only are they sucking your energy from you, but they are also wasting time and occupying a seat at the table that someone else should be sitting in.

SOMEONE WHO SHARES YOUR VALUES

The final necessary leg that supports your relationship with your TableMates is the values that you must share. We will go further into detail about what exactly we mean when we say "values" later on in the book. But for now, just know that sharing common values with your TableMates is a key factor to a healthy and sustainable relationship.

NO LEGS

The table around which you and your TableMates meet only endures if it has a sturdy foundation. If the legs are delicate, not installed properly, lopsided, or missing, we have a major problem. Shaky, unstable foundations lead to disaster.

We last left off with Sam when he decided he wanted to set about creating a Board of Directors. We gave him our advice and set him free. We met periodically during the next nine or so months. He updated us, and from what we heard, he was doing well. On the one-year anniversary of his efforts, we met and were shocked to hear stories about some of his TableMates. To be brief, his TableMates were unethical. We won't go into how Sam figured that out, but what is important is that Sam did figure it out. Sam admitted he threw our advice to the wayside. In his search, he got blinded by the wrong things. He got caught up in pursuing TableMates because of their images, extravagant lifestyles, and star-studded Rolodexes.

Sam was bothered by his missteps. We told him not to beat himself up. We all make mistakes. It is easy to be seduced by the image of success.

During our meeting, we worked with Sam to outline what aspects of a TableMate meant the most to him so that he could move forward in his search with those things top of mind. Below, you will find some of the questions we asked him. Use them as a starting point for your own search.

What are my core values? How do those values show up in my behavior?

Whose life story have I been most connected to and inspired by (famous or otherwise)?

How do I want to contribute to this world?

If I didn't have to worry about money, what would I do?

How has social media and technology blurred my perception of my values and goals?

How does my immediate environment impact my values?

After Sam answered these questions for us, we set a plan and let Sam free on his search for a whole new set of TableMates.

CHAPTER 7

Where to Find Your TableMates

Congratulations! You now have your ideal TableMate in mind. Now, we gotta go find him or her.

Some might consider this next part the "hard part," but we don't think it has to be. Yes, the process of bringing people to your table is definitely more difficult in the beginning (as all important skills are), but over time, it gets easier. For Meghan, once she understood what she was looking for, it took her about five months of actively searching to land her first new TableMate. From that moment on, everything got easier.

Let's get into it!

Before we talk about where to look for TableMates, let's talk about where not to go looking for TableMates. Remember, as with the advice from the previous chapter, these are rules and every rule has exceptions!

WHERE NOT TO FIND TABLEMATES
NETWORKING EVENTS

They suck. They are usually awkward and can feel forced. In our opinion, they are basically the professional relationship equivalent to speed dating.

One of Shari's seminar participants had this to say about networking events. "The thought of putting on a name tag and going to a networking event gives me heart palpitations. I'm just so awkward...so awkward. When I first started forcing myself to go to those events, I would meet someone and then stick to them the whole night; I used them like a crutch. I kept forcing myself to go, because I thought it would get better, but it didn't. Yes, I can get myself into some conversations, and I can get some contacts, but the nature of the event just isn't for me." We couldn't agree more!

At networking events, everyone is just throwing mud at a wall and waiting to see if it sticks. It's costly, time-consuming, and inefficient. It is directionless. It is everything we stand against in the quest for mentorship.

For the most part, unless you are highly, highly selective with what events you attend, networking events are pointless. Now, as with anything, there is a caveat. If you have a specific job in mind or a specific person whom you really want to connect with and who will be at said networking event, then go! Use your own good judgment here.

Unfortunately, many people go to networking events to give their card out to as many people as they can. They go to shake hands and kiss babies, but often, networking events don't lend the intimate environment necessary to make TableMates.

NETWORKING SITES AND SERVICES

We also suggest staying away from certain social media and "networking" sites. There is one particular giant (not naming names, but it rhymes with "DinkedIn") that is probably the most well-known of these virtual spaces. It is known for its services for job seekers, but the company has, as of summer/fall 2017, begun to haphazardly branch out into the mentoring game.

They've announced a Tinder-like mentoring feature in which you swipe to connect with a mentor who is on the service. In researching the overall response, we came across the following excerpt from an article on *The Verge*, and because we couldn't have said it better ourselves, we have included the following snippet.

> If it sounds a lot like a toothless attempt at winning over younger users with a design method borrowed from the soulless dating app paradigm of our time, you would be quite correct. Most mentorships in life arise from natural occurrences with bosses or colleagues or people who, over time, organically take on the role of someone who's looking after your career because they believe in you and think you're talented. LinkedIn, like a number of other venture-backed "coaching" services that are trying to commodify good advice, wants you to skip right to the awkward and unpleasant moment when you and another person must own up to the shallow, transactional nature of your relationship. And what better way to do so than by initially judging them at a glance based only on what your brain can glean from 10 seconds of looking at their face and highest-listed credential?

It's a "never-ending quest to connect you with other working professionals whom you will never again make contact with."[1]

We want to thank the author, Nick Statt, for putting it so eloquently.

Relationships built online through social networks and cold-emailing are just not sufficient. Not to mention the danger—we have your safety in mind here—that can come of it. Finding mentorship by way of reaching out to strangers, without a first introduction by a respected third-party, typically does not work. Yes, there are exceptions as always (lucky you), but in our experience, and in our extensive research, the TableMate you need will not be a stranger, or a stranger to anyone you know. Period.

In *Lean In for Graduates*, Sheryl Sandberg, the queen of tech and the COO of Facebook, likens courting strangers to mentor you to the plot of the children's book *Are You My Mother?* Basically, in the book, a baby bird goes off on a quest to find his mother. He asks a number of animals and even a couple of inanimate objects like a car and a plane if they are his mother. Of course, they are not his mother, and each says "no" or ignores him completely. This is essentially the same as asking a stranger, "Are you my mentor?"

In her book, Sandberg writes, "If someone has to ask the question, the answer is probably "no." When someone finds the right mentor, it is obvious. The question becomes a statement. Chasing or forcing that connection rarely works."[2]

Instead, find great mentors through the inspiring people

you're already interacting and working with now. You should source your TableMates from a pool of people to whom you've already demonstrated your potential and personality to in some way. They should have some sense of who you are and how you think, act, communicate, and contribute. And they have to like, trust, and believe in you already (why else would they help you?). They also need to believe with absolute certainty that you'll at least try to put all their input and feedback to great use.

Last, unless you have a personal connection to them, stay away from famous or semifamous people. They are more likely to say "no" to mentoring requests from strangers. Why? Because their time is already spoken for, and they're drowning in similar requests.

Shari often travels to conferences where she meets numerous high-profile, successful, and highly sought-after people.

She was at a conference abroad at which a unique business leader was in attendance. He is enigmatic and gregarious, and he seemed to have a gaggle of people constantly in tow. Shari noticed that people clung to him at meals and in-between sessions.

One day, while she was eating lunch at a table nearby this man, Shari heard him say something to the people at his table that was very surprising. According to Shari, he said, "It's normal for people to want to stay around me, and it's also normal for people to keep reaching out to me after we part. But don't. I won't be there for you in the way you will need me to. When I am here, I am able to help you understand my business world and hope to impart valuable advice. But when we go our separate ways, I can't do much more than to wish you well."

The people sitting at his table fell silent. They seemed shocked. Shari, however, was not.

Why wasn't Shari shocked? Because she understood the difference between a TableMate and a person who markets himself as a "speaker" and "mentor," who stands on a stage and speaks to thousands of people at a time and who doesn't know your name.

Shari wasn't shocked at what he said, but she was pretty impressed that he had the chutzpah to say something that honest. That man, after all, had built his reputation off of the idea that he could coach and inspire people to greatness. But he knew the limits of the persona that he had created. She respected him for that.

That being said, you can still approach public figures, just don't expect them to readily want to come to your table.

Shari has a well-known CEO of a global company at her table. The CEO has spent a great deal of his career working among millennials. Coincidentally, in her first book, Shari focused on customer service (and teaching it to millennials).

When they first met, he had opened up the opportunity to talk, and Shari took it; many others around her had not. When she introduced herself to him, she didn't gush or ask to take a photo together. She had carefully prepared how she was going to approach him. She knows from experience that you have about twenty seconds to capture attention enough to carry on a thoughtful conversation.

She did, it was an intelligent exchange, and she was asked to leave a copy of her book. As Shari puts it, the CEO showed class by sending her an email only days later commending her on her work.

That's the type of relationship Shari has with her own mentees, and it's a relationship she values. In this case, they do not have the opportunity to meet face-to-face more than once or twice a year, but they do connect through email, where Shari has been able to ask for advice.

This man is an exception to the rule. Shari and this man developed a trusting and respectful connection. He cares for Shari and has a true TableMate relationship with her.

But, to many famous people who pretend to be mentors to the masses, their followers are just another download of their podcast, a buyer of their newest book, a face in a crowd, and a voice in a void. They care about the results of their advice, but they don't care about the individual. How could they care? They don't know you.

One particularly famous man is guilty of this. He has successfully created a cult following, but his conversations with his "mentees" are one-sided. He talks *to* his crowds, not *with* them. He tells them the answers he has found in his own life, but that's the extent of the conversation. Some people are okay with that. They are happy to hear the secrets of the rich and famous and believe that if only they apply those secrets to their own lives, they too will be successful. But the relationship with a real mentor extends way beyond just a one-sided conversation!

So, where does this leave us? Be careful pursuing strangers, be leery of attending formal networking events, and avoid swiping algorithmically controlled mentor "dating" apps.

You might be asking yourself, "Well, for the love of Pete, where do I go to find these people?"

We got the goods!

WHERE TO FIND TABLEMATES

Look around you. Take a long look. As Shari says, "Start with who you know, and watch it grow."

Look to your preexisting relationships. Look to your friends' parents and your parents' friends. Look to your grandparents and their circles. Look to your coworkers. Look to the people you know through the activities you do after work and on weekends. Look to your neighbors. There may just be incredible value that you have overlooked.

Don't just look at those people. Look at who they may be connected with or related to.

When Shari first developed her workshop for millennials, she opened it up to the children and friends of people she knew. Those members brought others to the group and it grew steadily.

When you start with who you know, at some point, be prepared to step up, to ask questions, and dive deeper. It's a time of discovery. What if you were a closet poetry writer who always wanted to find out if your work was publishable? Isn't one of your core friends' parents the head of the local university's English department? Go over for dinner and open up a dialogue about it. Maybe your college roommate lives in sunny California, and you have really cool design ideas for surfboards that the people in Minnesota just don't have a market for. You just never know who the retired gentleman from down the street is, the one who never fails to stop and pet your dog. Strike up a conversation. Sound simple? That's because it is.

When Shari was first published in the business world, her kids' friends who were enrolled in business and commerce programs in university began ringing the doorbell. Every single one who did was invited to the table where they had many discussions. In turn, they invited Shari to speak during their freshman orientation week.

One relationship stands out. Saarim, a young man who recently earned his master's degree, reached out to Shari through social media to ask if she wouldn't mind meeting for a discussion. He was clear and respectful in his query and explained how he was connected to one of her kids' friends. Shari agreed to meet for a quick bite.

Saarim talked about his experience with turning an idea into a viable enterprise while studying entrepreneurship. He said despite his success, he felt "inexperienced and at a loss as to where to go next." He went to visit his family's home country and spent time "contemplating" and thinking about what he valued. He returned with a new idea and a plan. Saarim "found people to work with by connecting to people he knew and asking them to connect him further." His business was born.

Reaching out to Shari provided him with the opportunity to discuss his ideas. The "quick bite" turned into a two-hour lunch. Saarim left with insight and helpful tips and a couple of new questions to ponder. His wheels were turning, and his thoughts were spinning. In his words, he "did not know what to expect when [he] took the initiative, but [he] sure as heck was not expecting what did happen."

Start with who you know, and let it grow.

IN PERSON IS WHERE IT'S AT

It is all about finding TableMates in person. That's where true connections are made. That's why companies spend millions of dollars each year sending their salespeople on sales trips all over the world. Relationships are built face-to-face. When we interact in real-life situations, rather than through direct messaging or emailing, we let our guard down, we look people in the eye, and we have an opportunity to really ingratiate ourselves with the person across the table. Live and in person is powerful.

Getting started by looking around in your direct vicinity may sound intimidating, and it may be at first. But the good news is, often, once you start making your search known to the people around you, they will help you. They will introduce you to people within their own networks. They will remember you when speaking to their own friends. They will invite you to dinners, book signings, gala events—all of the boring things that they've been to a million times, but you haven't, and so it is exciting for you.

When you look to the people you know (or the people they know) for TableMates, think of it like you are tapping into a preexisting network. If it seems too daunting to go out and make new connections, all you have to do is knock on the door of one person you know, and you will be introduced to many more.

YOUR ORGANIZATIONS AND COMMUNITIES

Think about the organizations and communities to which you are already attached. For a lot of young people, a very obvious answer might be to look into alumni networks. This could be a great suggestion, but we are optimistically cautious about sending you there. Organizations like alumni networks may have events with "professional networking" overtones that end up feeling like networking events. If you do decide to look around there, try to do so without expectations that you will get anything back.

Think about the church you belong to, your book club, your baseball team, and the people you see every day when you grab your morning coffee, to name a few examples. Take the time to engage with them on other levels, discovering their experiences, passions, and values.

What if you don't belong to specialized or organized groups? You may consider volunteering in your community in something that really speaks to what is important or has a particular personal meaning to you.

From here, work outward. Workshops and seminars are fantastic places to be with others through specialized topics, ones that are of interest to you. It doesn't matter how small or grand, and pay particular attention when friends, relatives or associates speak about ones they have found.

Read the community news once in a while—you know, the one that gets left piled up on your doorstep before heading to the trash. Like we always say, you just never know. Begin around your own community and then move outward.

When looking for mentors within specific organizations, think about where you stand in said organization. If you are already a visible member who participates and knows a fair number of members, then go forth with your search. If you, however, are someone who hasn't really participated that much, think about how it might look if you all of a sudden appear inside a community and instantly start looking for mentors. It might ruffle the feathers of some members, because they might get irritated that you are using the community for purposes other than what that community is intended for.

Stella and Her Organizations

When we last left Stella, she was distraught over her "failed" meeting with a woman she saw as a potential TableMate.

We, of course, didn't see it that way and encouraged her to continue to meet with the woman. A year later, the woman and Stella are not TableMates. Yes, they meet occasionally and run into each other at industry events, but they are definitely not TableMates.

That is okay. We learned that that woman ended up introducing Stella to a group of women who meet regularly to talk about what it is like to be a woman in their industry. Through that group, Stella met two of her current TableMates! Because Stella became a part of a larger community, she has continued to meet more and more people whom she has invited to her table.

THE PEOPLE WHO ALREADY SIT AT A TABLE WITH YOU

Who has been in your corner in the past? Who has served as a reference for a job interview? Who has asked you for personal or professional advice? Who has sat at the table with you and encouraged you when you felt stuck? Who has praised you or encouraged you? Who has given you constructive criticism? Who is actually interested in the bizarre ideas and stories you like to talk about? Who also listens to your guilty-pleasure podcast about true crime? There are so many people in our lives whom we already have relationships with, be it professors, family friends, colleagues, random acquaintances, or friends of friends whom we haven't spent the time to see the potential in.

The point is that these people have spent time on you. If they've given you their time, they've opened up the door for you to ask for more. Yes, they may decline your offer, but the fact that the door was opened gives you the go-ahead to move forward with the ask.

Furthermore, as we said before, your best TableMate may not necessarily come in the box you expect. They might be a person who is already there, who knows you very well, and who is just waiting for you to ask the right questions.

Don't just see; "observe." Don't just hear; "listen." Learn to recognize an opportunity. Do not be afraid to say something or ask for a moment of someone's time. What do you have to lose? Nothing. What do you have to gain? Everything.

Who in your life is "perfect," and why? Are
your beliefs based on reality or perception?

—*Shari: Nobody! To be human is to be beautifully imperfect.*

Whom do you trust?

Whom do you respect?

—*Meghan: Those who don't let selfish*
motives impede the truth.

—*Shari: Those who give for the sake of the giving.*

PART III

Closing Is for TableMates

CHAPTER 8

Get Them to the Table

So, you've locked in on a potential TableMate. Now what?

March up to them, thrust out your hand, and strike a power pose. Just kidding. Please don't do that!

THE PRIMING PROCESS

We want you to connect and bring them to your table, yes, but before we launch into how to do that, there are some basic things you must be aware of.

Before you can establish a connection, you must prime yourself to being the type of person whose table a great TableMate will want to sit at. This relationship isn't all about them honoring you with their presence; you should want to also honor them with your presence.

As Stella moved through our process, when we got to this part, she laughed out loud. If she had been drinking water, we're sure she would have accidentally spit it all over us. "What could I possibly bring to the table?" she asked, incredulously.

Stella suffers, as we suffer and probably everyone suffers, from a lack of confidence in her abilities at times. We won't talk about where that insecurity comes from, but it's important to recognize and be honest with yourself about your insecurities.

In order to show her what she could bring to the table, we took her through an exercise. In this exercise, we dove deep into what we had observed to be her most badass qualities. We encouraged her to go out and ask other people who were close to her what they thought were her best attributes. Sourcing information from those around you is important, because often they see things you can't. Stella came back to us with the results, and together, we talked through each one.

At first, she didn't want to admit she thought they were right. She was reluctant to see the truth. We reminded her that the people close to her weren't lying to her. Eventually, through the meeting, she started to see— slowly at first—but eventually we broke through her skepticism.

Stella's friends and allies wrote over and over about her magnetic personality. We couldn't have agreed more; she electrified rooms. She truly has the ability to make anyone smile. She got really embarrassed when we brought it up. "I wish!" she said.

This interaction taught us the first thing about this priming process.

BE WHO YOU WANT TO BE

Even though Stella is charming and charismatic, she couldn't see it, and so she didn't believe it. Because we know you can't force someone to believe something, we tried a different tactic.

"Stella," we said, "instead of your friends and us trying to convince you that you are magnetic, how about we try something different? How about you try to convince yourself that you are magnetic for ten full seconds today. Repeat it in your mind, say it out loud if you need to. Eventually, up the ante. Practice thinking it for a whole minute a day, then for five minutes a day."

For so many of us, we just can't accept the great things that we offer. But, if we can push past that disbelief for just a second and keep pushing past it, then your insecurity will one day disintegrate.

When interacting with TableMates, be who you want to be, but first understand or identify what is important to you. At the table, you get the chance to practice on your future self.

Meghan doesn't have a five-year plan, but she knows she will have "made it" when she can throw a dinner party and have interesting, insightful, exciting, accomplished friends fill her dining room table. For her, that is the be-all and end-all. She practices for that future with her Table-Mates by being that person who has earned the right to be surrounded by incredible people.

LOOK BACK TO LOOK FORWARD

Think back to what you were like before the pressures of the outside world started pushing down on you. Who were you? Who did you want to be? Think back to the time when you didn't know limitations existed. Think back to the time when you were the fastest runner on the playground, and you took pride in being unabashedly "the best." Think back to the time when you didn't know any better than to say exactly what was on your mind. Go back to the time when you looked in the mirror without picking on your looks because you didn't even know what a standard of beauty was.

Revisit that person who was free to be.

Think about that inherent part of you that you left behind in childhood because you were afraid of its power. Bring it back, and let it ride!

BE THE PERSON WHO REACHES OUT

Text, call, email, send letters, send flowers, show up, and reach out. Be the person who is ready and available to make a lasting connection.

Sam has proven how good he is at getting TableMates, because he is a person who always reaches out especially when in-between physical face-to-face meetings. Sam makes a habit of keeping in touch with everyone who is important to him on a regular basis. He has grouped his network into three different groups: people he reaches out to weekly, monthly, and twice-annually. There is a special fourth group of his two most important personal connections whom he connects with daily or multiple times a day.

In-between his regular communications, Sam likes to stay relevant and at the forefront of the minds of his Table-Mates by sending them articles or interesting information that applies to their business or that they are personally interested in. For instance, Sam communicates with a former coworker by sending him videos of SpaceX rocket launches, because they initially bonded over their mutual love of rocketry. Sam also sends books that mean a lot to him to his TableMates.

Sam sets himself apart by taking the time to send snail mail. Sending letters is a lost practice, but everyone loves receiving a handwritten letter!

This keeps Sam accountable to all who matter to him. His efforts have paid off handsomely; he is so good at keeping connected that creating an even bigger network is a breeze for him.

Figure out how and when your TableMates like to communicate. Go ahead and ask them what their preferred method of communication is and then use that medium. Figure out when they are most reachable. Sam, for instance, is wary of taking the time of those TableMates who have young kids. He respects family time and never schedules dinners with those people on weeknights. That respect will go a long way.

Sam has also started hosting a dinner at his house every month or so. This is a great way to build stronger bonds because of the more personal setting. Dinners at home are really fantastic because there is no rush, no crowds, and no distractions!

Meghan Reached Out

I had always been a good student. But boy, college tamped that right out of me. During my sophomore year, I realized that my grades had taken a nosedive. It wasn't hard to figure out why. I wasn't participating in class discussions.

It's not that I didn't have anything to contribute. I didn't participate because I was terrified to speak in front of my peers and my professors. I felt completely paralyzed. So, I spent the next three years basically sitting silently in my chair.

When I was forced to participate, I found myself stuttering; I could not get the words out of my mouth. At first, I wasn't too worried, because it only happened when I was in class. But over time, that stutter showed up outside of class: when I was at work and with friends and family.

At that point, I realized I needed to take drastic actions. I signed up for a speech class and a drama class to force myself to speak in front of my peers. Those two things helped, but they weren't enough. So, I went back to the drawing board. I decided that I needed to push myself harder.

So, I made a plan. I would practice reaching out and talking to people through cold-calling. I made a list of interesting professors, business people, and thought leaders whom

I was interested in talking to. I spent a couple of months reaching out to them. I pulled the "student card" (people seem to be more agreeable to lending their time if you are a student), so they were much more willing to give me their time.

That practice was what finally launched me over the hurdle of my speech impediment. Of course, it still shows up from time to time, but overall, my life is so much better for the action I took. I even managed to make a career out of interviewing people!

I overcame my silent fear, and so can anyone else who is tortured by it.

Because I had honed the skill of reaching out, building my group of TableMates was that much easier.

BE AT THE CENTER OF YOUR NETWORK

In their book, *Connected*, Fowler and Christakis claim that where you stand in your network is one of the most important deciders of your status within the network. The more connected you are, or the closer you are to the center of the network, the more established and secure you will be in said network. An easy way to accomplish this is by connecting your connections with each other. That way, you are the central node between them.

Sam started to practice this, and once he did, he found himself in a completely different place with his Table-Mates. By connecting the people at his table with each other, he brought a lot of added value to their lives. He scheduled lunches with multiple mentors who had similar interests or were in similar industries and got them introduced to each other. His TableMates started forming relationships with each other, and now they can point back to Sam as the reason for it!

BE THE PERSON WITH FEW EXPECTATIONS

Last, when looking for TableMates, be very careful with your expectations.

Anyone worth pursuing a relationship with will typically have a full life. They have their own pursuits, their own projects, their own dreams. Do not come into this thinking that they will be easy to schedule time with. Sometimes, very busy people will have their planners filled out for months in advance. Do not take their inability to fit you in personally; that is just life!

It would be incredible if we could map out our perfect TableMate and 3-D print him out. But life isn't so generous. Yes, you will want to have a clear vision of the type of person you need, but you can't drill down so far as to become myopic in perspective. If you have too many strict expectations of your TableMates, you only hurt yourself because you keep your blinders on. This is not to say that you shouldn't have high expectations—you certainly should. But you can't have such strict expectations that you fail to see the possibilities in a different person who could potentially bring a lot more to the table.

GETTING BACK TO IT

Now that we've talked about priming yourself for success, let's get back to talking about how to bring potential TableMates to your table.

PERCEIVED VALUE

Perceived value is the value of a certain product in the mind of a customer. For instance, there are some people—maybe you are one of them—who make it a priority to have a really nice car. Other people, however, couldn't care less about the car they drive. They just want something that can get them from A to B. These different groups of people perceive the value of a nice car differently. The first group values what a very nice car can do for them, while the second group would rather spend their money elsewhere.

Perceived value extends past objects. People actually have perceived value as well. What does this mean? It means the way others see you is your perceived value.

This point may sound crude—it is. We aren't trying to lie to you. The way you market yourself, the way you are perceived, matters in the quest for TableMates. We want to encourage you to market yourself at a high value, so people will regard you as a person with high value. We do not mean you should lie. We mean you should assess what you already do and figure out ways to raise your perceived value.

Meghan learned this lesson from an idol of hers: Chris Sacca. In the early days of his career, he created The Salinger Group. It wasn't really anything other than a name on a well put-together website and all of his business cards. When Chris went out to find mentors, he referred to his company. Soon, people were saying that they had heard of his company.

The Salinger Group was nothing, but it made Chris appear to have clout behind him. The rest is history.

We suggest taking a little different route. For instance, let's say that you get paid to train and walk dogs. Instead of seeing yourself as a person who "walk dogs," think about yourself as a person who owns a dog-walking business. It is not a lie. You make money walking dogs. You are your business—own it!

Create a name for your company. Call yourself the

founder. Create a Facebook group. Get yourself a new email address with your company name in it. Not only will it help you get more business because you will appear much more legitimate, but it will also serve as a calling card when you are interacting with TableMates. You own your own business? Badass!

This strategy works for any small enterprise you run, be it editing resumes, babysitting, blogging, or web designing.

TableMates want to be around precocious, young self-starters. Silicon Valley has romanticized the young genius in a hoodie. Take advantage of the sexiness of youth in corporate America right now. Use your youth as a calling card for TableMates.

YOUR VALUE PROPOSITION

Let's dig a little deeper into perceived value by outlining how to understand your value proposition (or what value you bring to the table).

When approaching TableMates and getting them to the table, twenty-somethings must reiterate their value proposition to themselves and to others.

Understand your value proposition by answering the following questions.

What value do I bring to a relationship?

Where does my power lie?

What connections and experiences do I already have?

What skills do I have?

You might be sitting there unsure of how to answer. That is okay. But we guarantee that you have something to give. In fact, we know it.

Nicole had trouble understanding her value proposition. Nicole went into university not knowing exactly what she wanted. She held odd internships here and there. She ended up moving colleges in the middle of her four years because she just felt lost. Although she was unsure of her value proposition, she knew the power of action—she went out and pursued a half dozen different interests. Finally, over the summer of her junior year of college, she fell into her desired industry—video production. She felt so relieved because now she could apply her skills in a real way toward snagging her dream career.

She won a summer internship on an independent film and thrived in her work. She loved the intensely energetic and close-knit relationships she had while working as a crew member. After that summer ended, however, she had difficulty finding her next job. The competition for opportunities was intense, and all of her dreams seemed so far away once again.

But she remembered her value proposition—where her power came from. Her value lay in her education and her experience. No one could take those two things away from her. Day after day, she reminded herself of her value, and her confidence pushed the ball forward for her. She is now a part of a production program abroad. She found her value proposition and used it to leverage a job!

BE YOUR IDEAL MENTEE

Finally, whenever you're in a quandary about how to connect to someone, put yourself in their shoes. If the tables were turned, what would you want to see from an individual who wanted to connect with you? If you were inundated with requests for help every day, what type of person would *you* choose to assist, and why? Is your ideal mentee eager, insightful, helpful, fun, or interesting? Go out and become that person whom others would love to support and nurture.

Work hard at your job, show who you are and what you can do, help others, and demonstrate your value proposition.

GET THE INTERACTION RIGHT

When getting to know TableMates, getting them to your table will be much easier if you demonstrate the requisite respect they deserve.

Pay Attention

Pay attention. Get off the phone! If you really want to pursue success in a room full of people thirty years and older, put the damned phone away!

Swipe, swipe, scroll, scroll won't get you anywhere. When you keep yourself busy absorbing a deluge of useless content, you are wasting time. Instead, keep your head up so you will be prepared for anything.

In Aziz Ansari's book, *Modern Romance*, we can see how phone habits are a marker of your age. "When we did the large focus group where we split the room by generation—kids on the left, parents on the right—a strange thing happened. Before the show started, we noticed that the parents' side of the room was full of chatter. People were talking to one another and asking how they had ended up at the event and getting to know people. On the kids' side, everyone was buried in their phones and not talking to anyone around them."[1]

There is nothing that will make an adult immediately

jump to conclusions about your age like a blue glow on your face while in a room full of people! Put it away!

Listen

Listen!

Ask your TableMate what his story is and listen. Let him talk. Everyone likes talking about himself or herself. Give them the platform to do that here.

Michael, Shari's son, has been taught this from a young age. Often, when introduced to or conversing with older people, he will respectfully introduce himself, shake hands, look them in the eye, and then sit back and listen. He doesn't say much, but rather, he watches and absorbs. This helps Michael do two things. It allows his counterpart to open up a more intimate connection, and it helps him remember and internalize bits of treasured advice.

Listening is a lost skill. Stand out by flexing your listening skills. You will surely impress any TableMate.

Listening doesn't just benefit your TableMate; it can also benefit you in incredible ways. If you have found yourself among a group of great TableMates, what they say will be valuable.

Meghan listened from the start. She was willing to follow my advice and actually execute on what I had suggested. If I asked her to read an article, she had read it by the time I met her next. If I needed material or information for a specific project, she was sure to get those to me in a timely manner, and I never had to remind her!

Be like Meghan. Listen and then act! I assure you, it doesn't go unnoticed.

BE DETERMINED

If you are slow to make TableMates, do not panic. We expect a lot out of ourselves and expect things to happen quickly. Give your TableMates some time to come to the table.

We want a slow burn. We don't want your relationships to ignite, suck up all the oxygen, fizzle, and then die.

When you start talking to someone with power and experience, he will not open up to you right away.

Meeting for coffee for twenty minutes will not get you where you need to be. We think that is a misconception promulgated by the world of structured mentorship where you can go and meet someone for fifteen minutes and think you are making an impact. If you do this, neither side gets anything out of it.

Be consistent with your determination. Interact again and again. Stick to the relationship.

OFFER AND ASK FOR HELP

Offering to help and asking for help are scientifically proven methods to encourage bonding. We encourage everyone to start offering and asking for help.

Shari on Asking for Help

Even from the beginning of our relationship, Meghan asked me for help. I never felt put out when she asked, because she always asked for doable favors. One example I can remember was she was working on a book and needed help coming up with a title. Since I'm a *words* person, she asked me for help getting creative. It was actually a very fun exercise and helped us bond. I was flattered when she asked and realized just how much she trusted me with her work.

She also asked for simple favors like easy introductions to people I knew and for help with certain problems she was facing. I was happy to help, and I felt that it made our relationship stronger. Research shows that it actually gives us a better feeling toward someone when they ask us for help.

Meghan also delivered help in return. She introduced me to people in her network, she offered her opinion and advice (namely, with my own young adult children), and she brought a new fresh perspective that I so much enjoyed. I began to bounce new ideas off her to see her reaction. I trusted her with things I considered very private. Neither of us turned up a Shoulder when asking for help—we just wouldn't. It didn't mean we had all the answers but talking usually begat working the answers out.

Small things add up. You don't have to feel like you are changing lives—often that happens slowly over time—but small, everyday favors and help add up.

Small things add up faster when they are things that other people normally wouldn't do. Nobody likes doing menial, tedious tasks, especially if they are for someone else. Be the person who does them for people in your life and for your TableMates; they end up returning the biggest reward. For example, say one of your TableMates holds a quarterly meetup. Ask him if you can help set up or clean up after. Ask him if you can contribute food. At the meetup, introduce yourself to your TableMates' friends. Get to know people. Make the coffee for the meeting. These sorts of things are not hard, but you would be shocked at how few people do them and how much they are appreciated.

These small contributions are not limited to real life. You can help out and participate in your TableMates' lives online as well. Follow your TableMates' write-ups in journals or papers, or support them on their online communities like LinkedIn, a personal blog, Twitter, or any other platform. Participate in the online conversations they create and communities they frequent. Take action!

REMEMBER THEM

Remember whom you meet and what you spoke about. We recommend keeping written notes with the date, event, and names of people you spoke to. You can carry a small pocket notebook to write in or write directly on business cards that you may receive. If you have to or you prefer to, you can use your phone. But please do it sparingly! We don't want you looking like you're buried in your phone all night. If you do have to pull out your phone in the middle of a conversation to write something poignant down, please tell the person you are talking to, "Hold on one sec—I need to write that down." It's flattering and charming, and they'll feel like you are really interested and eager to learn.

By writing notes down, it will enable you to write more

personal follow-up emails, and it will help you start up conversations with potential TableMates the next time you speak. Recall a time when someone remembered something you said a while back. Didn't it feel good to have been listened to? Do that for the people you meet, and you will win instant brownie points.

A side note to this point: while you are keeping records, record your failures and successes. Did a certain story or phrase you told catch someone's attention? Did someone mention something interesting that you could share with others? Did a specific phrasing of an invitation to dinner work? Did you say something that was inappropriate or that caused you to leave the table thinking, "Why the hell did I say that?" Write it down! The only way we learn is from studying our mistakes.

BUDDY SYSTEMS

If you, like Meghan, are starting this journey with social anxieties, there is no harm in taking a buddy along when interacting with potential or existing TableMates. Showing up to events or high-pressure situations alone can be tough. Take a friend!

We don't mean for you to use your friends as a social crutch. Don't take a friend who will want to hang out in the corner or by the dessert table all night. Take a friend who is an asset. Ideally, this person will be someone who can hold a conversation, is interesting and interested, and puts you at ease. This person could be someone who also wants to create lasting relationships. That way, you two can work together toward a similar goal.

For Meghan, that person is her boyfriend. He can talk to anyone about anything, and that makes her feel less pressure to be "on." She can relax and let him lead the conversations while she warms up to people.

Make sure your buddy is okay hanging out solo if you muster up the courage to talk to someone and have to leave them alone.

It also helps if you set up a system with your buddy before you interact with others. For instance, if you get stuck in a conversation with someone you don't want to talk to, have a system in place for your buddy to come interrupt you and save you.

Buddy systems are not a sign of weakness. Your Table-Mates may also be people who prefer having a buddy. We are all human no matter how successful we are. Some of us just have issues connecting with others despite our best efforts.

Get your TableMates and potential TableMates to open up. Allow them to relax and enjoy themselves. No pressure, no deadlines, no work.

Many of our TableMates spend a lot of their days having to talk about a myriad of different subjects that they probably tire of. Let them talk about their passions and hobbies instead.

Don't make them feel like they have to take the lead or the authority position. Allow them to learn and be interested also. Allow them to lead the conversation to topics or stories that they want to explore.

The way you really connect is by letting the conversation flow and end up wherever it ends up. There is a time for lighthearted conversation and a time for serious discussion.

Give your TableMate the space to talk. Dorie Clark, the author of *Stand Out*, suggests asking open-ended questions. "'How long have you lived in New York?' is a decent question, but 'Why did you move to New York?' is likely to yield a much more interesting answer and new conversational directions."[2] Not only does this leave more room for the person you're talking with to talk about themselves, but it also gets back to moving from facts to narratives. To do that, you need to guide conversations toward understanding someone's motivations. The "why" is so much more interesting than the "what."

We worked with Stella on this skill. She was reluctant to get too deep or too serious. She had a tendency to want to keep the conversations limited to work or banal trivialities.

It wasn't that she didn't care to explore the deep stuff; it was just that she didn't know how to get there. Her go-to was asking interview-like questions and letting her TableMates talk endlessly about something they've been asked a thousand times before.

There was no give-and-take. Stella felt the consequences of that. She put herself into a corner where she wasn't able to open herself up to her TableMates.

She contributed too little to the conversations she had. She never got an opportunity to voice her opinions, feelings, desires, or interests. She presented herself as a totally boring person!

Meghan made this mistake in the beginning as well. She had a mentor who didn't know that she wanted to write. She just never mentioned it to him! It sounds crazy when she relives it, but she just never felt like she had the right to open up and share.

Luckily, Meghan realized her mistake and ended up telling him about her love of writing. It just so happened that he was friends with a best-selling author whom he was hosting a book launch party for that very night! He invited Meghan, and as she stood in his living room listening to that incredible author speak, she couldn't help but kick herself for not being open much sooner.

On the other hand, you do not want to reveal all of yourself too soon. Do not overload your TableMates with all your insecurities and dreams right off the bat! Save it for your best friends!

We have a friend whom we will call Tyler who is a big deal in his industry. He was introduced to a woman who wanted to break into that industry with her own business. The business itself was promising, and so Tyler agreed to help her out. When we heard about the woman's business, we figured Tyler would be a slam-dunk TableMate for her.

But it didn't turn out that way. Despite the fact that the woman had an incredible business, Tyler didn't end up helping her. When we asked him why, he said matter-of-factly, "Well, let's just say she sent me a message that was way too intimate way too fast."

Yikes.

It was a really bad move on her part, and she lost one of the best TableMates she could have ever hoped for.

Don't be that person!

TOO MUCH

If the process of bringing a TableMate to your table makes you overwhelmed, you can still get in the game while starting slow. We recommend taking a baby step. Ask someone (anyone!) who you think is cool out for coffee, a beer, a cupcake, or whatever. This person does not have to be someone you could see at your table. In fact, look for a person whom you know you don't want at your table, or whom you wouldn't be upset with if they didn't come to your table. This lowers the pressure by a lot!

Say something like, "Hey, I liked what you said about ___. I have some thoughts on that. Would you like to meet for a latte to talk about it?" No pressure, no longtime commitment. Just two people sitting down for a chat may be a good exercise to alleviating nervousness.

You never have to see that person again if you don't want to; it was just a practice round. If you still feel nervous, set up a couple of those low-pressure practice rounds to get yourself more comfortable with connecting.

THOSE WHO DON'T WANT TO SIT AT THE TABLE

What about those potential TableMates who reject invitations to the table? Rejection sucks. We all have been rejected before. The sting is sometimes unbearable—but in this case, don't let it be; it will save you a lot of heartache in the long run.

The people who reject invitations may do so for many different reasons. Perhaps they just got a big promotion and need to ramp up their hours in the office. Maybe they just had twins. Maybe they need to sleep seventeen hours a night. There are plenty of explanations.

If someone says "no" to you, do not take it personally. Remember that it likely isn't about you. There are many more opportunities waiting for you.

CHAPTER 9

The Ground

Sam and Stella had opened up to us desperately needing help. As with Meghan's coworkers, we couldn't just introduce them to someone like Shari and be done with it. We needed to educate them about the things we have found that work and the lessons Shari implements in her workshops.

So, we began by driving to the root of the matter for both of them.

We wanted to know their "why." We wanted to know what the motivating factor was for them to change their lives.

At the foundational level, Sam felt that he was locked in, trapped in his own life. He didn't like the path he was on, and he wanted out.

Stella felt locked out. She felt she was running around on the outside of the world trying desperately to get back in. She needed guidance in how to do so. Before coming to us, she mainly went to her friends for help. But Stella was getting nowhere because she was riding what we call the Starbucks Merry-Go-Round. Stella and her friends complained to each other about the same minutiae day after day without getting anywhere.

STEPPING OUT AND IN

To date, Sam is in a new job in a new industry. He has been working out and seeing friends. He is happier than he has ever been, and he is on a path that he feels in control of. His TableMates helped him get there. More on Sam later.

Stella, however, fell behind Sam. She still works as a nanny, but she nabbed a part-time internship at a music PR firm. She's getting there slowly, which is fine, but her journey has been more of a struggle than Sam's was. It wasn't that Stella didn't work as hard as Sam did. It wasn't that she didn't deserve the things Sam did. It wasn't as though she wanted it less than Sam did.

No, it was something more than that. Her journey was rockier because she wasn't primed in the way Sam was. Stella did not have the solid foundation that Sam had. Her foundational values were weak.

That is *no bueno*.

Your values are the foundation upon which your table stands. If you have a weak or nonexistent value system, then it doesn't matter if your table has all of its legs. It is going to wobble!

GROUND DOWN!

Everyone starts off at a very different point in the journey. But the very first step is understanding yourself and your values. Your values are the foundation upon which everything else lies; they are the ground upon which your table stands.

Values are intangible and often abstract, and so they may be difficult to understand. But really, they are just about the things you value. Spirituality, notoriety, money, comfort, religious faith, creative arts, caring for animals, creativity, education, and integrity are all values. What you value determines what you want, which determines your course of action. Check out our graphic below.

Realize your values, to realize your wants, to realize the actions you must take. Only then can you press the "doing button."

Stella didn't understand her value system, and so she didn't have clarity on what she really wanted out of life. Because she didn't know what she really wanted, she didn't know what actions she should take to get there. Because she didn't know what actions she should take, she didn't know how to get the right help from the right TableMates.

VALUES AFFECT THE TABLE
EXERCISE

Before we get any further, we want you to take some time to write down what you think your values are. Write them all down—the good, the bad, and the "selfish." There is no judgment here.

During this exercise, we recommend that you think of your values in three segments: values of your past self, present self, and future self.

Reflect on your life up until you started feeling stuck or lost. What did you value? This might be an embarrassing or discouraging exercise for some, but we all have times when we are embarrassed by the person we once were. That is okay.

Next, think about what values you currently hold dear. Once you make a list, go line by line and analyze your answers. Do you like what you see? If you don't, no worries. Just take note of the ones you are not proud of and move on.

Last, list the values you would like to see in your future self. It is incredibly important for you to be honest here. Shari often instructs her group to write as if no one but you will ever see it. Writing about what you think others will like is a waste of time here.

Think: what does that ideal person value? Once you have a list, you can consider this list your "core values." These are the values that will motivate you to figure out what you want and then take action to get them.

It is not an effortless process, but once you know your values, you will know what many call your "Big Why," or "North Star." The Big Why and the North Star are what we follow to get to where we want to be.

Let your values guide you.

IF YOU NEED HELP, SHARI'S GOT YOUR BACK

We lose sight of our values easily. That is because the rest of the world gets in the way. That's why I spend a lot of time in my workshops helping my students reach deep down to find their values.

I guide them in their search by using myself as an example. My two values are dignity and decorum. If you want to be saucy, you could call them the "Double D."

They have always been big with me and with my kids. I tell myself I don't care what kind of crap the world throws at you; you will conduct yourself with dignity and decorum no matter what. Those important values have stuck with me through many challenges in my life.

Naming your values is critical; it gives you a succinct visual for what direction you need to head toward in life, especially in respect to your career. Once my students have an idea about what their values are, I have them name them. Often, our values are esoteric, so naming them helps my students visualize and conceptualize them in a more succinct way.

VALUES CASE STUDIES

Below are stories of individuals whom we've interviewed, sharing how they have stuck to or strayed from their values and how that impacted them. These stories are meant to demonstrate how a single underlying value can affect wants and actions, how strong values produce strong results, and how weak or misguided values produce weak results.

GREG AND STABILITY AS TOLD BY SHARI

Greg is a friend of my family who used to come over to my house quite often when he and my son were in high school together. I always had tons of teenagers at the house looking for some good food to eat and a nonjudgmental ear to confide in.

Greg was different from the other kids. He was a good kid but was very quiet. He didn't open up like everyone else seemed to be able to do, but I figured he was shy.

Greg and my son, Michael, went off to college together and became roommates. One day during their sophomore year, Greg was abruptly pulled out of school and taken home. He was instructed that he was to live at home and work for the family business.

Greg basically dropped off the map for a year and a half. No one saw him; no one heard from him.

Then one day, with no forewarning, Greg showed up at Michael's dorm with two suitcases. He looked pale as snow and had lost a lot of weight. The next day, not knowing what else to do, Michael brought Greg to my house.

When I returned from a trip a few days later, Greg was still shaky and wasn't saying much. He couldn't look me in the eye, and he walked around forlorn and lost.

I finally found out (through Michael) that Greg had started self-medicating after he disappeared, and things in his household had deteriorated even further. Greg realized he needed to get out soon, or he may never be able to. It was now or never.

In the beginning, I sat Greg down and said, "All right, I don't know what's going on, but you're going to have to talk to me. For now, you have a place to stay. Remember, nobody is keeping you here, and you are going to have to look after yourself. You can make yourself comfortable in your own room in the basement. You are welcome to have whatever you want to eat—help yourself. But in return, you need to do some things for me. You're going to help me around the house and keep yourself and your room in a good state. This is going to be about mutual respect and taking care of each other." I then asked that he let his family know he was safe and working on himself.

He nodded his head, and replied, "No problem."

I let him be for the most part. He spent a lot of time alone in his room in the beginning. He was very reserved. But slowly and with consistency, I kept trying to break through his walls.

More than anything, I knew that whatever had been going on with Greg before, now he needed normalcy. He needed routine. He needed stability, and it had to come from taking ownership of himself.

I made a point of incorporating him into the regular routine in our house, even if Greg didn't volunteer to participate.

When I would have dinner ready for the family, I would call down to Greg and ask him if he was having dinner with us. He rarely showed up, so I left extra food in the fridge for him to have later. Even if he wasn't going to show up for a meal, at least he could rest assured that there was food waiting for him.

Days rolled into weeks, which rolled into months. The holidays were fast approaching. Christmas was right around the corner. I wanted to make sure Greg knew I was expecting him to be with us, and I subtly let him know that the holidays wouldn't impede our household stability.

I told him, "Listen, you're coming to our cabin and having Christmas." Very subtle, I know! In this request, as with certain things, I was not going to debate. The holidays are for the kids—any and all. By now, whether he liked it or not, he was part of the family and would be treated as such.

Greg agreed, and I made sure there were gifts for him.

We had a wonderful time. We went on our traditional Christmas Eve sleigh ride and ate too much food with lots of family around. Greg joined in on the festivities, and I started to see the light return to him. This, I thought, was a perfect way for him to see that everyone in the large, loud, and diverse family was there and cared for him.

Months passed and everyone, including Greg, settled into their daily routines all under one roof. Greg started to include himself in the daily household events. He began responding to the open conversations my kids and I had at the table. It's not hard to at my house! I think he was surprised that we asked him his opinion and were so open with each other. He saw that we all have voices and respect each other's opinions.

One day, he came to me and said, "Do you know someone who would hire me for a manual labor job?"

Shari said, "Yes, but if I make this call, you've got to be there, no matter what." I connected him to the gig and left the rest up to him.

It was a shitty job, of course, and he had to work twelve-hour days, six days a week, but he never failed to get up early every single morning and get out there. He had purpose, and I think it felt good to him to be productive and to earn his own money. He started eating more, working out with Michael, and taking better care of himself. His personality started to come back. He was on the up-and-up.

One day, a snowstorm hit. Greg and I couldn't leave the house, so we sat down and chatted. It was then that Greg finally opened up to me. He told me everything. I had known that Greg was in trouble and that he needed help, but I didn't realize just how few people Greg had in his life whom he felt he could talk to honestly.

Greg was dealing with a lot. He was lost, self-medicating, and wrestling with feelings of anger toward his family.

After I heard his whole story, I realized that Greg's opening up to me was inevitable. I saw that Greg valued stability because he had lacked it his whole life. What was I offering full-stop? Stability. He saw that I too valued stability, in the big things like keeping family close, and in the small things like making dinner every night.

He didn't have the word for it, but he saw in me a Table-Mate. Like clockwork, Greg opened up the floor for me to offer guidance and advice.

No, I wasn't a big-time player in an industry Greg wanted to be in. No, I wasn't the loving father that Greg wished he could have had. But I was the ideal TableMate for Greg, because I understood what he wanted and needed.

Now that Greg had invited me to his table, I set him on the track toward gaining the stability he so desperately wanted. In order to do that, I needed to teach him accountability and responsibility. Those two things would help Greg gain more agency over his life.

Greg responded with enthusiasm. He participated more in the family, and he helped out with anything we needed, especially garbage detail and walking the dog on rainy days, because that one always goes to the lowest one on the totem pole! He took care of himself and kept his room very tidy. Then, one night he came to me and said, "I won't be here two nights a week for dinner, because I enrolled in a night course." Boom! He was on his way!

He took his newfound internal stability and decided that he should take responsibility for his relationship with his father. When Greg initially came, he told me he would never see his family again. But months later, he had downgraded his statement to, "I will never live with my family again." I didn't say anything. I just smiled!

Greg arranged to meet up with his dad. I gave him advice

on how to interact with him in a self-respecting way. The meeting went as planned, and Greg has shown his incredible maturity through this new type of relationship.

Greg has transformed. He has a long way to go, but now he knows the formula. We started with his value. Greg valued, above all, stability. He didn't get it in his home life, school life, professional life, or personal life. But once he realized that it was what he so desperately needed, it gave him clarity on what he wanted.

He wanted a job that he could feel satisfied with. He wanted to be healthy. He wanted to have a mature relationship with his father, and he wanted to go back to school. This led him directly to action.

Greg just wanted to be a Canadian boy who remembered and embraced his family's European heritage, but who did not live under the old-school, back-home ways. He was now able to discern that, articulate that, and understand that he was the writer of his own story.

Greg is now supporting himself, living away from his family in his own apartment, taking care of his health, working a full-time job where he is respected, and exploring what other values he desires to live out.

I still reach out to him, because I want him to know my

support is steadfast, and there is nothing that is too difficult for us to talk about. I request that he comes over to dinner from time to time—after all, he signed up for the deluxe package!

INTEGRITY AS TOLD BY SHARI

I grew up in the sixties in a one-horse town in the desert of California. Sounds glamorous, doesn't it? If that didn't sound bad enough, I was one of five kids, and our parents were never around.

To say we were always hungry was an understatement. My poor eyesight resulted in my earning the nickname "Four Eyes" at the tender age of eight. Worst yet, we called the local motel "home." Cue Norman Bates.

You could say that because of our circumstances, we were branded, sort of like with the hot iron used on cattle, from the get-go. We didn't have any control of how the world perceived us, and life was difficult because of it.

There are plenty of things I don't remember about those days, and I hope those memories never resurface.

But there is one memory that I will never forget. It directly led to my adopting one of my first and most important values.

There was a family who lived down the road from us. They were solidly middle-class, but to me, they were rich! They had two daughters, one who was in my class at school, and one who was in my sister's grade. We all became friends.

This story takes place one Halloween night. Because the neighborhoods in the desert were so sparse, it was impossible to trick-or-treat. So our friends' parents—we'll call them Ward and June—took their daughters and my siblings and me to the local 7-Eleven.

Ward and June invited all of us to choose one thing from the store. We could choose absolutely anything! They threw their arms out wide.

If you knew the sixties and seventies, then you know the cornucopia of goodies that 7-Eleven housed. I can see the yards (which felt like miles) of confections in all their glory, without all the up-do packaging and aisles crowded with loud cardboard advertising. I can still smell the bubble gum and jawbreakers in the penny-candy bins. I can still see the little sugarcoated fruit pies, not the fake ones they make today, calling to me.

My siblings ran straight toward the candy. But not I. No, I turned and said one word to June, "Anything?" She proudly nodded to me. "Anything."

Naturally, I needed to savor this moment. I was not going to waste an opportunity like this like my siblings had by running straight to the candy! I strolled the aisles checking everything out. I stopped in front of the giant soda pop fridge.

I heard Ward calling me back to the checkout where everyone was waiting for me. So, I grabbed a bottle of pop. But I didn't grab the small personal bottle. I grabbed the family-sized one.

Once back at their home, where we were invited to have some Halloween party fun, I poured myself a glass of soda, and the bottle went into the fridge.

When it was time to go, I ran back toward the kitchen to get my soda pop. As I reached the fridge, Ward and June came out of nowhere and put themselves between the kitchen and me.

"No," they said with matching stares, "we are just going to leave the rest of the bottle here." Their once wide-open arms were now crossed.

I stood very simply and said, "Oh, yes, I guess we can have it some another time. I'll leave it here."

Even at such a young age, I immediately understood what

was happening. It was very, very clear to me that they were going back on their word; they never really meant what they said back in the store.

But what, then, was their original intent in saying that to us? Their intent was only to look like the heroes, not actually to be heroes.

How did they feel okay sending a child away from their home feeling like a fool when it wasn't even her fault? How did they manage to have less grace in their actions than an eight-year-old did? It was just a soda pop, but to a kid, it was everything in that moment.

One of my most important core values was born on that day. I call it "What Is Right and What Is Good." I act on this value, I always teach on this value, and when in doubt, I always fall back on this value. You can call it "honesty," you can call it "truth," but what it really is is "integrity."

It has served me well in many areas of my adult life, both professionally and personally, and I always practice it when I sit at the table, whether it is mine or anyone else's.

MICHAEL AND INDIVIDUALITY

Michael needed clarity in his life. At university, he studied economics, which he did well enough with. But the problems arrived when Michael started looking ahead on the typical economics student path. The next step was finding a big summer internship, that if all went well, would translate into a job, which would eventually become a career.

All of Michael's classmates who were also studying business in one form or another were planning on taking internships in banks or a number of other financial institutions. So, Michael followed their lead. He too applied to a couple of those sought-after positions, and he nabbed a coveted spot.

Everyone around him was buzzing with excitement to start their careers in business, but something about his future just felt wrong to Michael. He didn't know what it was, but he had an uneasy feeling in the pit of his stomach whenever he thought about the long hours he would have to sit in front of an Excel spreadsheet.

He turned the internship down. His friends couldn't understand why he would do that. Some even called him "crazy," but he was sure it was the right decision. What he was not sure of, however, was what the hell he would do instead.

But Michael preferred that sometimes unbearable feeling of uncertainty to the idea of suffering in silence while doing something he hated.

During this time, Michael turned to his TableMates. He needed clarity about what he valued. He thought he had valued competition and esteem, but his recent actions spoke a different story.

"It's quite obvious to me," one particularly blunt TableMate said to him one day, "that you value individuality. In that vein, you need to forge your own path forward. Following the predetermined route is just not going to cut it for you."

"I get that," Michael replied, "but I'm finding the alternative is hard."

"Yeah," his TableMate replied, "but you value individuality above a lot of other things. You can see it in your track record way before this. Of course, it's easier to stay on the path, but it will do more damage than good because you fundamentally are opposed to it."

What his TableMate was saying was that he needed to live his values at whatever cost. With that confidence in mind, Michael started figuring out what else he valued.

He made a list that he shared with us: individuality, helping others, health and wellness, polished professionalism, and family.

Michael used those values to inform his new internship

search, which led him to working a marketing and customer service job at a health-and-wellness institution.

Because his path aligned with more than one of his values, he loved what he did.

Because Michael clarified, identified, and named his values at a crucial point in his life, he is better able to understand how and what he wants. Because he knows what he wants, the actions he takes are specific and are executed with confidence and conviction.

STELLA, WARPED VALUES, AND THE PARADOX OF CHOICE

Michael got with his TableMates and defined his values. He was able to get clarity because he understood that a value system was important, even if he didn't know exactly what his values were.

Stella, on the other hand, was never taught about the importance of values. Because she was never taught that, she never knew that her foundational values were...well, nonexistent.

By her account and the accounts of those closest to her, Stella's value structure had rotted. By no means did that signify she was a bad person. All it meant was that she was floating because she had no anchors.

She grew up on a diet of reality TV. Her parents were good parents, but they were emotionally absent. She did not try in school and was not encouraged by her mom and dad to get good grades. So, she didn't. She had spent her time trapped on what we call the Starbucks Merry-Go-Round. All her problems, all of the things she was worried about, and all the emptiness she felt was funneled through her shallow conversations with her friends. Figuratively, they would gab and complain about their shallow pains over burnt lattes while going round and round on a merry-go-round that they never wanted to leave. Complaining and not doing anything day after day was the easier way to deal. So, like Stockholm sufferers, they preferred to stay trapped.

But when things came to a head for Stella after she found herself aimless after college, she knew she needed to get off that twisted carousel.

"I'm a loser," she told Meghan one day in utter frustration. "I peaked in high school. I don't even know who I am or what I care about. I know where I want to work, but that means nothing if I don't know who I am."

Stella was convinced she had reached her upper limit. But she was wrong. What she needed was to discover her underlying values, which would then enable her to shift her desires, which would then enable her to act to get where she needed to be.

Instead of scrolling through Instagram in her spare time (which she confessed made her "depressed"), she should start exploring the things she truly loved. We asked her to start small. Because we knew she really did love the music industry, we suggested she start following music bloggers and music industry news sites.

It was the small steps that would lead to great changes for Stella. We worked with her for a long time, going through what her value system actually looked like. We knew it would evolve over time, but if we could get her acquainted with the basics, she would be in a much better position to interact with TableMates and have clarity in her actions.

She came to us discouraged through a lot of the process. Her fake values had manifested in unfortunate side effects like an eating disorder, extreme anxiety, and a nasty habit of obsessing over her image. She sought counseling for all of the above and more. The counseling focused on eliminating those false values, and we worked with her on replacing them with true values.

Once Stella got aligned on her value system, her search for TableMates got a lot easier. For instance, she realized that she did value friendship, but she had never picked healthy friends. So, through establishing relationships with Table-Mates with whom she felt respected and empowered, she was able to go out and satisfy her need for great friends in a healthier way.

Everyone has the ability to make a change at any time in his or her life. TableMates can help you do that, but you need to put in the work to understand your values first.

Stella is on the right path and is taking strides toward her future.

SAM AND COMMUNITY

Conversely, Sam knew what his values were, but only after he had failed and brushed himself off first. For the second go-around, he wanted TableMates who were intelligent, who valued truth, and who were there to offer Sam a community.

He was the type of person who thrived in social situations. You could say he was like a golden retriever puppy: 99 percent extrovert. He needed people around him!

He realized that that was what he was lacking in his post-college life. His boss didn't care about him, his friends were dispersed, and his family was trying but missing the mark. He knew, though, that what he needed was a network of people who could catch him when he was down and help him raise himself up. He, of course, wanted to do the same for them.

On his second go-around searching for TableMates, Sam sought out those people who he could see also valued community. They were the people who were leaders, helpers, and people of service.

They opened their arms up to him and were eager to help him on his quest.

You might think Sam's journey ends with him getting a new job, but it doesn't. He did get a new job through the recommendation of one of his TableMates, and he was able to land a position that offered much more mentorship and growth opportunities, but Sam's journey is really just beginning.

He understands, now, that when he pursues his values, not only will he be more satisfied in life, but he will also be involved with people who hold those same values.

NICOLE AND PASSION

Nicole didn't always know what she wanted to do in life, but once she did, she didn't let anything get in her way. She was fiercely passionate about storytelling and art, and so naturally, she wanted to be involved in film production.

Her passion was palpable to those who worked with her. She was the first one at the filming location every morning and the last one to leave. She asked everyone, "What can I do to help you? What do you need?" She was on her feet, going and going for upward of sixteen hours a day.

Yet, she still felt stuck. The industry is very difficult to break into. She felt as if she was outside of a party ringing the doorbell and no one was answering for her. She could see everyone on the inside; she just couldn't get there.

A TableMate of hers, who recognized the incredible power of passion, told her to just keep chugging along and do what she was doing. Passion breeds success, and if you value your passion, success will come.

It did come, but it didn't come out of nowhere. It came because people noticed her work ethic. On her first ever full-length independent film, Nicole blew the crew out of the water. On that project, she proved herself. She got to show her chops and also met a couple of new people whom she now knows and loves and who know and love her.

Through the good word from those connections, Nicole got introduced to a woman producer who had heard all about her. Nicole barely needed to interview for a job—because of her reputation among her network, the female producer took her in with open arms.

She pursued Nicole because she was a proven entity.

Believe us when we say that talent is hard to find. If you can prove yourself as talent (i.e., a hard worker, a team player), you will be sought after.

It's easy if you have passion, but it can just as easily be done through consistent and persistent action, and a bit of working your ass off.

SHARI AND HIGHER LOVE

Shari suddenly found herself at a crossroad. She had just divorced her husband and business partner of twenty years, and on her fiftieth birthday, she found herself alone.

She was sad, yes, but she wasn't sad about that chapter of her life ending. She was sad that this new chapter—the chapter of her—had started so late in life.

She had been living someone else's dream for so long. She loved her business and her family life, but what she really wanted to do was express her creativity through the arts. She wanted to teach, share her famous recipes, and write books. She wanted to finally give attention to her most overlooked, but important value: her higher love.

Your higher love value is the thing that gives you goosebumps when you think about it or talk about it. It makes your heart thump loudly in your chest. It makes you feel bigger than yourself.

But often, we keep our higher love hidden from the world. We store it away from the world out of shame and embarrassment because we feel like our higher love is unreachable. And what if we were to try to go out and get it? We might fail! That failure might lead to humiliation or pain.

We can't think that way. We must lean into our higher love to make our lives deeper and more meaningful.

Shari has two higher loves.

Her first higher love is feeding people. She went through times in her life when she had literally nothing to eat. At that time, that type of poverty was stigmatized. She knows firsthand just how debilitating it is. She knows what it feels like to be told that you have failed society, failed school, and failed yourself. Later in life, when she finally had the means, she opened up her home to kids in her neighborhood so that they could get as much healthy food as they needed. Now, she has started a foundation to help feed hungry children. She wants to care for them when they can't care for themselves.

Her second higher love is bringing art to life and telling

stories. She does this through writing books, holding seminars, and producing movies.

Shari, like many of us, had put her higher loves on the shelf and became really good at making excuses as to why she couldn't pursue them.

But now she is happily pursuing them full-stop.

Some have come to her and said, "Well, isn't it a bit too late for that?"

Shari just smiles back at them and says, "It is never too late."

It is never too late.

Shari has a friend—we'll call him Gary—who took a vacation in Switzerland. Gary is in his fifties, but he is in excellent shape and had planned on hiking while in Europe. On one of his treks, Gary was completely out of breath and doubled over on the side of a steep trail. He heard someone walking up the trail behind him at a surprisingly brisk pace. "Man," Gary thought to himself, "whoever that is must be a major athlete."

Who rounded the corner on that steep trail but a tiny, fragile, ninety-something-year-old man. He, unlike Gary, was completely fine—no huffing and no puffing.

Gary asked him, in-between breaths, "How are you not out of breath? Have you been doing this all your life?"

The older man didn't even stop and said, "No, sir. One day I woke up, and all I wanted to do was hike this mountain. So, every morning, I do just that!"

His age didn't matter. Scaling that peak every day was his higher love, and he had no qualms pursuing it with vigor. It became easier over time.

It wasn't too late for that man, it wasn't too late for Shari, and it certainly is not too late for you to find and pursue your higher love.

FINDING YOUR HIGHER LOVE

We often reveal our values without even recognizing it. Want to spend all of your holidays at home with your parents? You probably value family. Do you devote your weekends volunteering? You value charity and giving. Are you the biggest sports fan you know? You might value spirit and group bonding.

We may not know it, but what we do and what we like reveal our values just beneath the surface.

But the higher love value is often buried far down; for

some, it's as deep as the Mariana Trench. Your higher love is sometimes the hardest to pull out of you, but it's essential that you do. That is because it is the value that, above all else, if we don't explore and express it, we may end up feeling like Shari did: that we are living someone else's life.

For Shari, the revelation of her higher love value didn't come all at once. It came slowly once she started getting the right people at her table.

Our hope for you is that you start on the process of unearthing your higher love. For some of us, you may be aware of it and comfortable talking about it. But for others, Meghan and Shari included, it takes time, confidence, and effort for it to come out.

One of the best resources in this process will be your TableMates. When you have the right people sitting at your table, discussions about higher love are bound to happen. Begin by talking to your TableMates about their higher loves. Some might be hesitant at first to discuss them. Show your genuine curiosity and don't pry. They may have stories about higher loves they pursued. Others may have stories about higher loves that they never pursued.

Here are some questions that may prompt the conversation:

Have you ever thought of something that you believed you'd never be able to do? Have you ever done it?

What if you could? If you could do anything you wanted, no parameters, no bars, no limits, what would it be?

What are you passionate about? What do you care about in life?

What is your biggest insecurity? What gives you goosebumps?

What do you dream of doing?

The vulnerability you see from your TableMate when he opens up to you about his higher love may help you feel comfortable opening up too.

Shari met a twenty-something named Grace who invited her to come sit at her table. Grace was struggling with her higher love. She told Shari, "What does it even matter? I have so many more years to figure it out. It's too far down the road to even contemplate." She explained to Shari that she felt like her real life was just out of sight—like it existed around a corner. But instead of Grace just being able to look around the corner, she couldn't see the other side because the corner was more of a curve that seemed to never end. Her higher love lived around that curve that she couldn't see the end of, so she decided she just wasn't going to think about it.

There are a number of reasons why Grace might have felt this way. Maybe she was afraid of the enormity of whatever lay on the end of that curve. Maybe it was too much work; being "stuck" was more comfortable. Maybe her higher love was too big for her to feel okay confronting.

We're here to tell you your higher love is never too big, and it is never not worth pursuing.

Shari said, "Stop right there. Yes, that is true. Life isn't a corner where you take one step and you are on the other side. It is more of a curve, and you never know where it ends. But that doesn't mean you just stop searching for your higher love. Put on your damned running shoes and go find it!"

If you can't run, that is okay. Take a small step and have the confidence of knowing your TableMates are behind you.

We're better together, so let's stay that way. Find a place where you can just be yourself and where your values are brought forth.

FIRST OR LAST RESORT

Meghan began her journey of finding her higher love in earnest after she graduated from college. Her first step was an unusual one. Instead of getting a fancy job, she worked at a summer camp. At that summer camp, all of the counselors have to pick a counselor name, which they have to go by for the whole summer. It's really interesting because the counselors will leave camp with some of their best friends for life, but sometimes they don't even know each other's real names!

That summer gave Meghan the opportunity to search for her higher love because she was in a completely new place with a completely new set of people with a completely new name. Meghan saw this as an opportunity to let go of her anxieties and hang-ups and just be the person who she wanted to be. She had a chance to reset, clear the brush, and figure out what exactly made her tick.

She found that she actually really enjoyed this new person—this person who she had always wanted to be but just never thought she could be. That summer was the launching pad on Meghan's journey to her higher loves of travel, writing, and helping others.

We can't recommend this sort of *tabula rasa*, blank slate experience enough. Of course, not all of us have the opportunity to do such a thing. But you can get the same effect through less drastic action. All you have to do is put yourself in a situation where no one knows you.

You can start a new hobby, join a group, go on a solo vacation, get a pen pal. The point is to put yourself in a situation where you don't feel pressure to be the person you always have been. Allow yourself to step into a situation where no one knows you and see who comes out of you. You might really enjoy that person, and that person might show you where your higher love is!

PAY IT BACKWARD

When you get on your path (and you will!), and when you start managing that curve, stop for a second and turn around. Notice who is lagging behind you. Are your friends struggling? Are your siblings suffering? Once you commit to running this curve toward your higher goal, you will have the power to help others do it as well. Share your journey with them, inspire them, be real with them, and sit at their table with them.

In what area of life would you like to inspire others?

What are your values? What are your wants?

What happens when you press the "doing" button?

—Shari: Magic happens, regardless of success.

—Meghan: I suck it up, close my eyes, and get it done.

What are you going to do?

Conclusion

In Zen Buddhism, there is a term called Dokusan, which means "going alone to the respected one." When practicing Dokusan, the student goes to the teacher to ask questions and talk about his journey. These meetings are meant to be informal sessions where the "teacher" assesses the student's progress toward mastery. Often, the session devolves into a hodgepodge where the imploring student asks the "master" over and over again how to achieve whatever given objective they are struggling with at the moment. They just want the secrets.

Therein lies a trick.

Students travel from all over the world to study under Zen masters. They come to temples asking to be taught. They stand outside begging to be let in. Often, the masters will turn them away at the threshold day after day.

But if the hopeful student demonstrates persistence, the Zen masters will finally entertain his requests.

"What do you want from me?" the Zen master will say.

The student will respond, "Please let me come in. I wish to learn from you."

"Why do you care to talk to me? I don't know any more than you know."

"Yes, you do," the student will say. "You are a Zen master, after all."

"I can't teach you anything, but I see that you will not leave, so come in."

The student thinks he has been granted entry to the secrets, but the master knows otherwise.

Some students will go on practicing Dokusan until the cows come home, thinking it will get them further along in their journey toward the secrets. The secret is, it won't.

The masters, although exalted for their wisdom, do not have the secrets. That is the whole point; they can't help the student since they are only students themselves. Once the student realizes that, he frees himself from the construct of "student" that he alone chained himself to. But as long as the "student" is looking for an answer—as long as he continues to treat his teacher like he is all-knowing—the student is not ready.

Only when the student demonstrates an honest, truthful connection, stops treating the master like he is higher on the hierarchy, and speaks to the master like a friend rather than a teacher, the student will release himself from his constant feelings of being "lesser than."

The student can't gain the secrets, but what he can gain is a community of like-minded individuals who support each other in the tireless search for truth.

That is the true beauty of the communities of Zen masters living together: they search together, support each other, and sit at the table together.

Love from Shari

You are capable of so much; you have such a great capacity for good.

At the same time, I see you scared, stuck, and searching. It's okay to feel this way—many do.

Don't feel alone.

Admitting you need support is part of gaining maturity, folks.

We're better together, so let's stick together.

I know I couldn't have done it alone, without my Table-Mates. They inspired, enlightened, and cheered for me. They kept my sometimes-wild streak in check, sat next to me, and helped me up when things got rocky. They listened to my hours-long phone calls where I rambled on about my doubts and fears and my trials and tribulations. They laughed with me while I jumped on the bed in an excited frenzy. Quite simply, I couldn't have done it without them.

Lighter and Brighter

To be human is to feel the weight of the world. As we grow, we experience the weight differently; we gain a new perspective every year that we are on this earth. The most incredible part about bonding to others is the ability to see this world—with all its pain and with all its wonders—from a different perspective.

When the weight of the world gets heavier, and time seems to slow, your TableMates can offer you the support and the perspective of age that will give you hope and make everything feel a little bit lighter and look a little bit brighter.

Trust them, care for them, and love them.

TableTalk us at tt.tablemates@gmail.com.

Giddy up!

About the Authors

 **SHARI MOSS** is an author, entrepreneur, executive film producer, and adventurous warrior. Her current focus is conducting workshops and creating inspirational information to help millennials achieve their maximum potential. Shari and her two children currently divide their time between Toronto, Canada, and Austin, Texas.

 **MEGHAN FITZPATRICK** is an award-winning author, editor, and ghostwriter of ten books on topics ranging from personal development to business process management. Raised in California, she studied international politics at Georgetown University and, after an extended period of traveling, has finally settled in Austin, Texas.

Notes

INTRODUCTION: TAKE A SEAT

1 Hill, Amelia. "The quarterlife crisis: young, insecure and depressed." The Guardian. May 05, 2011. Accessed February 09, 2018. https://www.theguardian.com/society/2011/may/05/quarterlife-crisis-young-insecure-depressed.

2 Marcus, Mary Brophy. "Job satisfaction in your 20s and 30s may impact your health later." CBS News. August 23, 2016. Accessed February 09, 2018. https://www.cbsnews.com/news/job-satisfaction-in-your-20s-and-30s-may-impact-your-health-later/.

3 "MILLENNIAL UNEMPLOYMENT RATE STAGNANT AT 12.8 PERCENT." Generation Opportunity. August 05, 2016. Accessed February 09, 2018. https://generationopportunity.org/press-release/millennial-unemployment-rate-stagnant-at-12-8-percent/.

4 Alton, Larry. "Millennials Are Struggling To Get Jobs - Heres Why, And What To Do About It." Forbes. December 22, 2016. Accessed February 09, 2018. https://www.forbes.com/sites/larryalton/2016/12/22/millennials-are-struggling-to-get-jobs-heres-why-and-what-to-do-about-it/#2ed6a7d84bb0.

5 Gene Smiley. "Great Depression." The Concise Encyclopedia of Economics. 2008. Library of Economics and Liberty. Retrieved February 9, 2018 from the internet: http://www.econlib.org/library/Enc/GreatDepression.html

6 Stahl, Ashley. "New Study Reveals That Millennial Underemployment Is On The Rise." Forbes. May 18, 2016. Accessed February 09, 2018. https://www.forbes.com/sites/ashleystahl/2016/05/18/new-study-reveals-that-millennial-underemployment-is-on-the-rise/#12a334356e5f.

7 Payout. "The Underemployment Phenomenon No One Is Talking About." Forbes. September 28, 2017. Accessed February 09, 2018. https://www.forbes.com/sites/payout/2017/07/21/the-underemployment-phenomenon-no-one-is-talking-about/#721408c75a01.

CHAPTER 2: GENERATIONAL GAP LEADS TO GENERATIONAL HATE LEADS TO GENERATIONAL GAP

1   "15 Historical Complaints About Young People Ruining Everything." Mental Floss. August 15, 2013. Accessed February 09, 2018. http://mentalfloss.com/article/52209/15-historical-complaints-about-young-people-ruining-everything.

2   Reeve, Elspeth. "Every Every Every Generation Has Been the Me Me Me Generation." The Atlantic. May 09, 2013. Accessed February 09, 2018. https://www.theatlantic.com/national/archive/2013/05/me-generation-time/315151/.

3   Simon Sinek, Excerpt of Simon Sinek from an episode of Inside Quest, *Simon Sinek on Millennials in the Workplace*, YouTube, Published on Oct 29, 2016, https://www.youtube.com/watch?v=hER0Qp6QJNU.

4   "Suicide Statistics." AFSP. Accessed February 09, 2018. https://afsp.org/about-suicide/suicide-statistics/.

CHAPTER 3: WHY WE SHOULD COME TO THE TABLE

1   Nicholas Christakis and James Fowler, *Connected: The Surprising Power of Our Social Networks and How They Shape Our Lives—How Your Friends' Friends' Friends Affect Everything You Feel, Think, and Do* (New York: Little, Brown: 2009).

2   Keith Ferrazzi, *Who's Got Your Back: The Breakthrough Program to Build Deep, Trusting Relationships That Create Success—and Won't Let You Fail* (New York: Crown, 2009).

CHAPTER 4: THE TABLE

1   "Board of Directors," Wikipedia, accessed September 14, 2017. https://en.wikipedia.org/wiki/Board_of_directors.

2   Staff, Investopedia. "Board of Directors - B of D." Investopedia. December 18, 2017. Accessed February 09, 2018. https://www.investopedia.com/terms/b/boardofdirectors.asp#ixzz4yFzMYqDM.

CHAPTER 5: THE SHOULDER

1   Jeffrey Pfeffer, "Can Nice Guys Finish First?," *Harvard Business Review*, December 2011, https://hbr.org/2011/12/can-nice-guys-finish-first.

2   Revolvy, LLC. "'Cold shoulder' on Revolvy.com." Trivia Quizzes. Accessed February 09, 2018. https://www.revolvy.com/main/index. php?s=Coldshoulder&item_type=topic.

3   Meg Jay, *The Defining Decade: Why Your Twenties Matter—and How to Make the Most of Them Now* (New York: Hatchette Book Group, 2012, 96.

CHAPTER 6: THE RIGHT PEOPLE AT THE TABLE

1   Andy Weir, "The Egg." Accessed February 09, 2018. http://www.galactanet.com/ oneoff/theegg_mod.html.

2   Condoleezza Rice, director of Stanford University's Graduate School of Business's Global Center for Business and the Economy, and former U.S. Secretary of State.

CHAPTER 7: WHERE TO FIND YOUR TABLEMATES

1   Nick Statt, "LinkedIn's Latest Millennial Bait Is a Tinder-Style Mentorship Service," *The Verge*, August 3, 2017, https://www.theverge.com/2017/8/3/16091418/ linkedin-tinder-mentorship-microsoft-advice-coaching-feature.

2   Sandberg, Sheryl and Nell Scovell. Lean in: for graduates. New York: Alfred A. Knopf, 2016.

CHAPTER 8: GET THEM TO THE TABLE

1   Aziz Ansari and Eric Klinenberg, *Modern Romance* (New York: Penguin, 2016), 41.

2   Bellis, Rich. "How I Learned To Stop Hating Networking Events (Mostly)." Fast Company. May 06, 2016. Accessed February 09, 2018. https://www.fastcompany. com/3059531/how-i-learned-to-stop-hating-networking-events-mostly.

Made in the USA
Middletown, DE
02 August 2019